RANSOM

The Medical Mystery That Stole Our Son and the Fight to Get Him Back

Hope Shepherd and Jack Shepherd

ISBN 978-1-63814-574-5 (Paperback)
ISBN 978-1-63814-575-2 (Digital)

Covenant Books
11661 Hwy 707
Murrells Inlet, SC 29576
www.covenantbooks.com

Dedicated first and foremost to God who, in His perfect timing, keeps His promises.

Also to Dr. Miroslav Kovacevic, the angel in the white lab coat, who gave us our son back.

Finally, to my sons, Jack and TJ, whose resilience inspires me every day.

1

TAKEN

Even though I walk through the darkest valley, I will fear no evil,
for you are with me; your rod and your staff, they comfort me.
—Psalm 23:4

I wish I could pinpoint the exact moment my son, Jack was taken.
I know it was right around his third birthday, but it's impossible for
me to report with any accuracy the life altering second the kidnapper whisked him away while I was staring at him, as yet blissfully
unaware.

It's every parent's worst nightmare: a child snatched from the
periphery of your vigilance. Once I realized he'd been taken, I did
what any parent would do in this gut-wrenching situation. I searched
for him. I called in the professionals. The response was a mix of confused looks, raised eyebrows, and the occasional tasteless smirk. What
do you mean, your child's been taken? He's right there.

And he was. When Jack was taken, he never left the house. To
the outside world and even those closest, he looked like Jack. How
could I blame them for not believing my panic? The only physical
feature that gave it away was Jack's eyes. His sky-blue eyes, clear with
calm plus a hint of mischief, were wide, cold, somewhere else. Jack
was somewhere else, but I was the only one who knew it.

I didn't know where Jack was or who had taken him. All I knew
was I put my sweet, quiet, gentle, inquisitive boy to bed one night

and woke up with a completely different child. As the years went by, Jack came back, sometimes for days, weeks, or even months, until he was stolen away again.

When Jack was with me, I savored the moments. I held on to him as he fell asleep and held my breath when he woke. Which child would I get today? Every beat of my son's heart was etched in my memory from the time he'd grown under my own. Jack was the dream baby who slept four hours at a stretch the first night home from the hospital and switched seamlessly between breast and bottle. Jack was the contented toddler who reached for my hand crossing the street and tagged along on errands without a single protest. He was the preschooler who beamed when he saw my face and proudly presented me with macaroni necklaces and newly mastered sight words.

The red-faced three-year-old hurling books at my face was not my son. Jack was not the six-year-old lifting a kitchen chair over his head like the Hulk and hurling it clear into the other room. My child was not the nine-year-old losing the ability to scrawl a legible sentence.

But where was Jack, my Jack when this other child, this stranger, was inhabiting his body? Was he stuck somewhere, trying to get back? Why had he left, and more importantly, how could I get him back?

2

IN THE BEGINNING

I prayed for this child, and the Lord
granted me what I asked of Him.

—1 Samuel 1:27

September 16, 2008

I screamed. My husband could sleep through a train rumbling down
the center of our bedroom. Again, I screamed for him to *come here
right away*. Maybe not the best way to communicate with someone,
especially if said audience is in the REM cycle, but I was in a state of
shock. I stared down at my hand. Couldn't be.

"What's wrong? What is it?" Luke stumbled into the bathroom,
one arm flung against the door frame, his face a mixture of groggi-
ness, confusion, and concern.

"I'm pregnant." I brushed my hand over my stomach, smooth-
ing my baggy pajama shirt.

"What? No, you're not."

I waved the stick at him. "Yes, I am. Look. There's two pink
lines."

Still partially asleep, Luke grabbed the box on the bathroom
counter and studied the glossy instructions. His sea-glass blue eyes
alternated between the instructions and the stick in my hand. I
watched the cautious excitement light his features.

"It could be wrong," he said, always the realist, needing to see replicated results in black and white. Or pink.

I shook my head, my black hair falling in my face. I needed a haircut. Before long, I wouldn't have much time for such frivolities—and I couldn't be happier. "It's not."

"Hope, this one could be faulty. Take another one."

I produced the three other pregnancy tests I'd taken. Don't ask me why I had multiple pregnancy tests lying around or what made me take one (four) in the first place. I honestly don't know.

Luke sighed and a flash of annoyance permeated my excitement. Why wasn't he jumping for joy? Well, I guess I could answer my own question. Luke was an accountant. He never jumped for joy.

"Hun, you know what the doctor said. I mean, you haven't even had a cycle since she took you off the pills. She told you this couldn't happen, not without intervention. I know how much you want this. I just don't want you to get your hopes up."

I stared back down at the test. "Don't you want it?"

Luke brushed my hair out of my eyes. "Of course. But I don't think I can believe it until we get confirmation from the doctor."

"Fair enough. I'll go in tomorrow."

"How did this happen?" I asked my doctor after she produced said confirmation. I flushed. "I mean, I know *how* this happened, but you said…"

She put a hand on my shoulder, warm through my T-shirt. "I have no medical explanation for you."

I thought back to the night of my initial appointment, the night I'd knelt by the side of my bed for the first time in years and prayed for a baby. I prayed for all the women whose hearts were filled with preparatory love while their arms remained empty. I still do.

I don't know that I'd ever experienced true elation before. The closest was probably when I removed the lid from a gift on my sixth birthday and uncovered a wriggling Lhasa Apso puppy. I paced our cozy townhome, babbling about the size of the baby compared to fruit, baby names, and baby supplies. Always the information junkie, I obsessively consumed pregnancy message boards, books, and articles. Once the honeymoon phase passed, anxiety began contaminating the excitement. Well, that and nausea.

What if something I ate, did, or smelled hurt the baby? The on-call nurses barely suppressed a sigh at my inane questions and panic that something might be wrong. My doctor told Luke to "keep her away from Google."

My typical intimacy with anxiety was deepened by my desire for this baby, my gratitude, and my nagging guilt. Why me and not one of the countless others who were waiting for a baby? I wanted to be worthy of becoming this child's mother and protect him. Suddenly, it was all that mattered. I still thought I could control everything. If I did everything "right" my child would be safe.

*****

After my dad lost his arduous battle with lung cancer, my mom said it's good we don't know what's ahead because we couldn't face it all. I think she's right. I'm glad I didn't know that keeping my child insulated and healthy would be like harnessing the wind.

No matter what I did or how diligently I prepared, the storm would come.

3

BEING JACK'S MOM

When anxiety was great within me, your
consolation brought joy to my soul.

—Psalm 94:19

June 1, 2009

Jack was born on a muggy, drizzly day in June, six days before his
due date and three weeks before my twenty-sixth birthday. It was the
last time we'd ever be early for anything! He was seven pounds and
healthy.

Yes, my fears during pregnancy proved unfounded, but needless
to say, that didn't banish my worries once we brought Jack home.
Watching Luke pull the car around and loading Jack in the back seat
for the first time, I thought, *Wait, they're letting me go home with this
human who I'm now responsible for keeping alive? Why did he say "good
luck"? Wait, the nurse isn't coming with us?*

Luke peeked in the rearview mirror before exiting the driver's
seat and opening the back door. He reached over and adjusted the
lime green "leaf" mirror we'd attached over Jack's rear-facing five-
star safety rating car seat in the middle seat. Jack's room (and our
modest townhome, by this point) was adorned in jungle theme. This
cute reflecting leaf with a smiling monkey face in the corner pre-
served our theme and allowed us to check on Jack in the rearview

mirror. Cautious prior to becoming a dad, my twenty-four-year-old husband drove home on the back roads, our reliable, hand-me-down Toyota RAV4 passed on the right by grandfathers in their Buicks and Cadillacs.

"How's our son doing?" Luke asked every few minutes.

I couldn't stop staring at Jack's little face. *Our son.* I was reminded of the previous summer and the jolt of excitement I got signing "Mrs. Shepherd" and finding reasons to say "my husband." My sense of déjà vu lingered as Luke and I carried our son over the threshold of our first home. Just over a year prior we'd sat on the kitchen counter and poured five-dollar champagne into the sixty-dollar crystal champagne flutes from our wedding shower and toasted winning the bid on our townhome. (The glasses are long sense broken, and we paid above asking price right before the market crashed, but that's another story.)

I loved the all the natural light, the blue, yellow, and green walls, the balcony looking out on the pond. Walking in with Jack allowed me to see these things as if for the first time. Everything seemed... new. To this day it's one of the things I love most about parenting— the gift of experiencing what's become mundane as new and exciting all over again with your child.

We proudly showed Jack his room because three-day-old babies appreciate faux wood flooring and jungle décor. Our cats sniffed Jack, offered us a bored look, and went back to lying in the sun. We transferred a sleeping Jack into his crib and stood side by side looking at him like, "Now what?"

Everything down to the fresh batteries in the mobile was set. I was all ready for motherhood, but wholly unprepared. Sure, I was young, but I don't think anyone's ever prepared to become a parent. I figured I was because, you know, I'd worked as a nanny in college, which is the *exact same* thing. Also, I have a degree in psychology. Couldn't hurt. Nonetheless, all the firsts were equal parts exhilarating and terrifying. The first day Luke went back to work when Jack was almost a week old, I had to stop myself from blocking the door. The first pediatrician's appointment offered both relief and uncertainty.

And of course, I'd learned that my all-nighters in college had nothing on the chronic sleep deprivation of motherhood.

I was told over and over again by family members, friends, and random elderly ladies in church that Jack was an easy baby. I had no basis for comparison at the time, but for the most part, he was. He was content to ride in his stroller watching the world. He settled easily and started sleeping through the night at six weeks old. "You've no idea how easy you have it," seasoned mothers would tell me. At the time, I resented it because hey, being with a newborn twenty-four hours a day isn't always easy. They were right, though. I had no idea how simple life was and how little power I had to keep it that way.

Jack blossomed from a dream baby into an agreeable, happy toddler. He spoke in sentences by eighteen months, wrote letters and read sight words at two, and potty-trained by two and a half. I could take Jack out running errands for hours with hardly a fuss. We did mommy-and-me classes, story time, zoo trips, and playdates. I met some great fellow moms, and we bonded over the sometimes-isolating world of staying home with a toddler.

I was often lonely in those early years; Luke worked long hours and travelled frequently. I came to rely on our weekly outings and interactions with other moms. Jack wasn't a big napper, so I filled our days with invented errands and enriching (or at least time-consuming) activities. I was coasting along, figuring out my life as a mom. I felt confident in my role. After all, look how well-behaved my kid was. Another lesson would break through my naivete: good parenting doesn't ensure good behavior. Right around Jack's third birthday, this lesson would literally smack me in the face and knock me spiraling from my pedestal into a six-year roller coaster journey more harrowing, heartbreaking, and hopeful than I could've ever imagined. We celebrated Jack's third birthday in June of 2012, the summer when everything changed.

4

BEAUTIFUL DAY, DARK NIGHT

*My brethren, count it all joy when you fall into various
trials, knowing that the testing of your faith produces
patience. But let patience have its perfect work, that you
may be perfect and complete, lacking nothing.*

—James 1:2–4

Monday, October 22, 2018

It was a beautiful day in fall. The Midwest is stingy with its pleasant weather. I savor fall days when the oppressive humidity has worn off like the excitement of a once-anticipated Christmas gift, and the chill hasn't yet claimed the air. I had high hopes for that day.

It was Monday—one of the two days per week Jack attended fourth grade at his hybrid school for homeschoolers. The remaining three days a week we completed lessons at home. Homeschooling—just one more landmark I hadn't foreseen on my parenting journey. Not that I had anything against it; it was never on my radar.

TJ, our five-year-old, was off school and anticipating some coveted one-on-one time, plus two dogs. He'd been asking to go to the dog park. TJ shared my passion for animals. While Jack loved the dogs and enjoyed petting other dogs at the dog park, he lost interest quickly. TJ could spend all day there. Our favorite dog park was close to Jack's school. Having two children with special and often conflicting needs was breeding ground for guilt. Having one child homeschooled and one in full time kindergarten, I often lamented about the need for more one-on-one time with TJ. It was a perfect day for TJ and I to visit the dog park.

After spending a few hours at the dog park, TJ and I had lunch at the café across from Jack's school. We ate outside on the dog-friendly patio, fighting the aggressive yellow jackets as they reacted to impending winter. I was weary from having my arms pulled by excited dogs, but the day's generous weather and Jack's buoyant morning mood begged a walk on the trail by our home. I retrieved Jack from school with high hopes.

*****

"Hi, Jack, how was your day?" I asked as Jack dragged his back-pack into the backseat.

He flopped in the seat and sighed. "Fine."

I glanced at him in the rearview mirror. His dark hair partially obscured his eyes. His jaw was tight. He glanced over at his brother in the seat next to him. "Stop it, TJ!"

"Jack, your brother's not doing anything," I said. My heart sank.

"He's *looking* at me and *smiling*."

That was all it took. TJ laughed. It wasn't just a laugh; it was the chuckle he reserved specifically to annoy his big brother.

"You are so annoying. Stop it, TJ!"

"Okay, Jack, move to the backseat, please." Thank God for third-row seating.

"Oh my gosh, why do you always blame me for everything? I didn't even do anything. He started it!" He jabbed a finger at TJ, who helpfully laughed in response.

I felt my heart in my stomach. I mean, it literally sank. I blinked rapidly, afraid tears of disappointment would escape. He'd been fine this morning, hadn't he? He hadn't even complained about going to school.

"I didn't say you did anything, Jack. I just think it's best if you and your brother don't sit next to each other right now. Did you have a long day at school today?" I said, trying to go with empathy.

"No." Jack shuffled into the back seat.

Once he was buckled, I put the car in drive. TJ rolled down his window. The cool breeze and the buzz of other cars entered the van. I cracked my own window to counteract the pressure building in my ears.

"TJ, close your window!"

"No!"

"Close it now!"

"No."

"Jack, it's a really nice day. Why don't we—"

"You always take his side. He gets whatever he wants."

"I get whatever I want, Jack!"

"Close your window, TJ. You're so mean."

"Hahaha."

I closed TJ's window and locked it.

"Thanks, Mom."

"Mom!" TJ said. "Unlock my window right now! You are so mean!"

"No, TJ," Jack said, suddenly calm.

"You're not the parent, Jack!" TJ announced, repeating a reminder I often used.

"Boys, can we just drive home and not fight over the window?"

"Pavlov is sad! He wants the window open but now he can't because Jack's so mean. You're so mean, Jack."

I'd forgotten the dogs were in the car. "TJ, don't call your brother names. We had a nice day together. Now we're going to go home and take a walk on the trail."

"Noooooo!" Jack wailed.

I passed a semi. *I hate trucks*, I thought, redirecting my frustration at this neutral target.

"No what, Jack?" I sighed.

"I was just at school all day. I'm tired. I want to go home and play online with Austin."

I wavered. Jack was obviously in a state. But I couldn't always placate him. He'd been sitting all day, and he needed exercise. Besides, I couldn't get over the idea that we were on borrowed time, weather-wise.

"You can play with him after our walk while I make dinner. We won't be gone long. You'll have plenty of time."

"No, I told him I'd play when I got home!" When Jack made plans, he assumed everyone else was on board.

"Well, we can't just sit on the computers all the time. It's a beautiful day." For some reason, I thought continuously reiterating the beauty of the day would cajole the boys into a compliant mood. It was another act of desperation. As a depression sufferer, I knew all too well that a walk under changing leaves on a beautiful fall day wasn't enough. In fact, the weather was mocking us. *Don't you wish you could enjoy this day like a "normal" person?*

The drive to the parking lot backing up to the wooded trail took less than five minutes. I opened the trunk to retrieve TJ's bike.

"Don't open the doors until I come around. We don't want Pavlov to get out," I told the boys. Waverly was timid and stayed close, but if Pavlov saw an opening to escape a game of chase was sure to ensue.

I managed to wrangle both dogs and keep a grip on the hood of TJ's jacket while he walked his bike through the parking lot.

"I'm going to win the race, Ja-ck!" TJ announced.

Jack glared at me as though I was the one who'd uttered the antagonistic words and stomped after his brother.

I tried. I tried to appreciate the kaleidoscope of swirling leaves and the crunch of the dry ones under my Sketchers. I was trying too hard. Part of me knew my effort was futile.

The dogs spotted a group of geese and dragged me down the dirt trail. Jack stormed after his brother's bike like a missile. The tree-lined path led to a playground. TJ skidded to a stop and turned his head back to look at me. Sweat glistened on his pale forehead under his Lightning McQueen helmet.

"Mom, can we play at the park?" His blue eyes shown with excitement. TJ was still at an age where every playground offered a new experience no matter how many times we'd visited it.

"Ugh! Parks are boring. I'm hungry."

I frowned. Jack was typically the first to recommend a trip to the park on a nice day. "Just for a little bit, Jack. Then we'll go home for dinner."

I squinted at the sky. The light was already softening. This was about the time I'd start anticipating Luke's call from his office, letting me know which train he'd catch on his way home from the city. I looked forward to the relief and reconnection of that call and Luke's homecoming. That night Luke had a work dinner, and I didn't expect him home until well after the kids' bedtime. I'm not sure other parents experience a sense of sadness and anxiety welling in their chest at a spouse's travel or late nights in the office. At least, no one talks about it. For me, the loneliness of managing behavior and tiptoeing over eggshells through a minefield made me long for the presence of my partner and someone with whom to share the extreme parenting. Don't get me wrong; not all days are like this one. In fact, days like the one I'm describing allow me far richer joy and appreciation for the good days. The days where Jack's eyes and mind were clear. The days where my boys' relationship was filled with games and giggles rather than physical and verbal pokes.

But if I'm being honest, I spend every day plagued with a fierce and unrelenting imposter syndrome. Too often, I feel like a child playing the role of a grown-up, waiting for the legitimate adult to show up.

I tied the dogs to the cool metal bench bolted to a slab of cement, turning around in time to witness Jack beating his brother's beloved bike with a thick stick. Defeated, I wondered how I'd get through the remainder of the day. Taking a deep breath, I stared up at the pink-blue sky and fought back tears. I collapsed onto the cold red metal bench. My cell phone buzzed in the pocket of my black windbreaker. I nearly dropped it in my haste to answer my husband's call.

"Hello?"

"Hi. Sweetie, how's your day going?"

I swallowed hard before answering. Selfishly, I wished Luke would come home to be with me. I wished his dinner had been cancelled. I blinked rapidly.

"Okay. Jack's having a rough day," I said under my breath.

The threat of tears was about more than loneliness and a desire for my husband to come home. The truth is difficult to admit. It's harder to document with words. The truth is, on that day and many others I was afraid of Jack. I worried for the safety of TJ and myself. I was afraid of my own child. My nine-year-old.

"I'm sorry, hun," Luke said. "What's going on?"

"I don't know." My voice sounded whiny. "He was good this morning. We're on the trail now—Jack, no! You could really hurt your brother." I leapt off the bench, startling the dogs. TJ was teetering on his bike while Jack—sweet, gentle Jack was jabbing a twisted stick into the spokes of the bike. The clanging and honking symphony of the city leaked from the phone into my ear. I reached for the branch. Jack jerked it beyond my reach.

"All right, hun, I'm at the steak house. I'll let you go."

Again, I held back tears. "Okay."

Luke could no longer hear me. He said goodbye. I could just make out the sound of him greeting a coworker before the line cut out. I pictured them clad in business casual, shaking hands, and discussing red wine options.

TJ shrieked and started peddling back the way we'd come. Jack let out what can only be described as a growl and charged after TJ, wielding the branch.

"Stop!" I yelled to both of them, pursuing Jack. I got close enough to snag the back of his jacket. In a Houdini move, he shrugged out of it. The dogs barked frantically behind me. Fortunately, they were the only observers. I lunged, managing to catch hold of Jack's arms. He pushed back against me. I stumbled but managed to latch on to the stick and peel Jack's hands from the smooth bark.

"Jack, you could hurt yourself or someone else!"

"I don't care."

I knew that wasn't true. Jack, my Jack, cared deeply, about everything.

"TJ, wait," I called. My youngest had gotten better about staying close to me, but I still couldn't trust him to not keep going without a backward glance. TJ braked by dragging his feet in the dirt, allowing me a sigh of relief. He looked back at us.

"Jack's gonna hit me!"

"He won't." Gripping Jack behind the elbow, I marched him the ten feet or so back to the dogs. They lunged at the end of their leashes. I didn't even remember putting the stupid stick down.

I struggled to untie two large dogs with one hand while keeping a firm grip on Jack with the other, swiveling my head around like a cartoon character to make sure TJ was still in sight.

Jack stopped struggling. "Mom, can I have your phone," he said, eerily calm.

I attempted to replace my spine with steel. "No, Jack." I measured my tone. "We're walking back to the car now. You're not walking with your face in a phone." Obviously, his behavior didn't warrant privileges, but I was in deescalation mode. I knew from experience pointing this out would prove ineffective at best, explosive at worst.

I slid the loops of the leashes over my wrist. "Go ahead, TJ."

"God, just let us get home," I silently prayed. *"Please help me to make it through this day."*

Jack jerked his arm free, the nylon of his red windbreaker slipping through my fingers. "You're mean!"

"Jack, we're walking. Let's just get home." I headed down the path on autopilot.

"You're *so* mean. Stop it!"

"Keep it up, and you'll lose your computer," I said before I could stop myself. Knowledge didn't always halt emotion. My patience was wearing thin.

"I don't care!" Jack kicked at the gravel, making a big production of stomping and huffing down the trail.

I constantly wrestle with how to discipline Jack, and when. In this state, he was motivated by neither reward nor consequence. What did motivate him? What hadn't we tried? The removal of screens, his escape, led to him flying into a blind panic and becoming physical. Time-outs became a power struggle. Even talking and reasoning couldn't penetrate his fog when we were in this state. He was unreachable. It had taken me years to understand (and I still didn't fully), but when we reached the point of no return, he *couldn't* control his behavior. Reversing a train would've been easier.

*****

The remainder of the evening is a bit of a blur. Somehow, I executed the insurmountable task of preventing TJ from peddling out into the parking lot and getting two dogs, two kids, and a dusty bike back in the car. I know I stood outside the door for a few moments, staring up at the mocking blue sky. At home, Jack's mood darkened along with the sky. He vacillated between calling me mean and glaring at me, tight-lipped. By that point, I don't think either of us knew the origin of his anger toward me. Two tall whicker stools adorned the corners of our dining room. Jack dragged one to the middle of the kitchen, climbed onto it, and sat there holding a sign stating, "Mom is MEAN! ☹ I'm not talking to her," just in case I hadn't caught on.

I worked around him, making dinner, trying to get dishes into the dishwasher and the floor swept in anticipation of my exhaustion. I usually hit a wall around eight, like my body and brain have an automatic off switch. The tougher days shut my emotions down like an automatic survival mechanism. Every so often, Jack would vacate his perch and wave the sign in my face. I envisioned swiping it out of his hand and ripping it into pieces. This adulting gig is no joke. TJ contributed by screaming about something.

Finally, bedtime rolled around. We completed baths and showers uneventfully. Like the monkey reaching for the peanut after being shocked, I dared to envision the three of us laying in the boys' double bed, me squished between them, reading *The World According to Humphrey*. Hope goes out with boxing gloves on.

We used to call them meltdowns, the "episodes" during which Jack becomes destructive and violent. Jack goes into a blind rage, left with little to no recollection of the event. Now I know the term "rages" more accurately describes these episodes. The only possible course of action is to keep everyone (and everything) safe and wait out the storm. We know it's over when the tempered glass falls from Jack's beautiful eyes, and the rage literally drains from his body.

This night was one of the worst. I wasn't surprised, yet shock overtook me. No matter how many times I experienced the warzone of a rage, shock still accompanied it. Afterward, I'd wish I'd had the wherewithal or the opportunity to film it for the doctor. Reiterating it doesn't capture the terror of the event.

It happened after Jack's shower. I'd gotten TJ into his rocket ship pajamas and was attempting to cajole Jack into his flannel pants and Minecraft shirt.

"You're mean!" Jack screamed in a voice not his own. We were in the boys' bedroom, TJ flipped through books while I held the pajama pants toward Jack, who crossed his arms tightly over his chest in response.

"Come on, Jack, just put your pajamas on and we'll read. At least the pants."

"Ohh, Jack's in trou-ble!" TJ sing-songed from his seat on the bed.

Turning his back on me, Jack lunged for the bed. I intercepted him. He whipped around in my arms with an animalistic scream. I stared into his eyes, desperate to reach him. His eyes were cold and detached. Rearing his head back, he spit in my face.

We were in full rage mode. I glanced helplessly at the door, wishing I could magically summon Luke home. Jack weighed over ninety pounds. It was on me to keep him and his brother safe. Giving up on his pajama pants, I managed to pull him into bed, my bad back protesting with every maneuver. I tossed the Minecraft comforter over him and threw one arm and leg over his writhing body. With my free hand, I felt around for the Bible tossed amongst the tangled blankets. I flipped to a random verse and began to read. Jack's eyes rolled in his head, and he spit over and over again. TJ had gone quiet.

"It's okay, TJ," I said over Jack's shrieks. "Your brother's having a tough night." Understatement of the year. If I didn't know better, I'd think my sweet boy was possessed.

Jack shoved against me and shimmied under my arm and bolted for the bedroom door.

"Mom, what's wrong with him?" TJ asked in a small voice, as though my heart could break any further.

"He'll be fine. I need you to stay in here."

I darted after Jack, closing the bedroom door behind me. The bathroom door across the hall was closed, and I heard the metallic click of the lock. Luckily the old door didn't latch all the way. I couldn't leave Jack unattended.

"Jack, open the door. It's not safe."

"No! Go away." His voice was robotic. I heard his tongue clicking repeatedly, punctuated by throat clearing.

I pushed the door. Jack opened the top drawer of the vanity, effectively blocking my entrance. I managed to wedge the door open enough to squeeze my arm through and jiggle the drawer shut.

"No!" Jack lunged at me, nearly slipping on the navy towels that had been strewn on the floor. He shoved me in the chest, knocking me back against the wood door. He attempted to dart past me, but I grabbed him by the shoulders and spun him toward me. It was the fatal blow to my composure.

"What is wrong with you?" I cried, getting down to Jack's level and searching his eyes. I regretted the words as soon as they left my mouth, hating myself for directing that question at him.

Jack's eyes widened, fat tears leaking from the brims. The fog lifted. I watched the shock replace the rage. I watched the shine return to his eyes. His body went limp. He collapsed into my arms.

"I'm sorry. I'm sorry, Mom. I don't know why I do this. I don't know why. I don't mean to. Please help me stop. I don't want to be like this. Please help me. Please."

I cried along with him, holding him tightly and repeating how much I loved him and telling him it wasn't his fault. My own words, *"What's wrong with you?"* blared in my mind, torturing me. But still, the question lingered. Something was very, very wrong.

Nothing prepares you for the day your child breaks down sobbing and begs you for help. Nothing competes with the searing pain of not knowing how. Moms are supposed to have the answers, but how do you fight an invisible adversary?

I held Jack until he fell asleep and then I let my own tears fall unabated. Luke arrived home after ten finding his wife a bigger mess than the house. I tearfully recounted what had happened.

"I'm sorry," he sighed. "I don't know what to do anymore." Luke provided. He worked with numbers, and he was good at his job. He managed people decades older than him, solved problems, and put out fires daily. This unseen force was foreign to him. The helplessness suffocated us.

"I asked him what was wrong with him," I wailed. "I yelled. How could I say that to him? He'll always remember it."

"No, he won't. You're the most patient person I know. You were being attacked. You're human, and you have your limits. Besides, it broke him out of it." Luke unfailingly knew what to say to halt my self-flagellation.

"That doesn't make it okay."

"Hun, you're too hard on yourself."

"I just want him to be okay. I don't know how to help him."

"I know." Luke rubbed my back. "Me too. You're a great mom."

*****

After Luke fell asleep, I slipped back into the boys' room. Their blankets were flung on the floor on either side of the bed. I covered TJ first, tucking in his black, gray, and yellow road blanket around his knobby shoulders. His eyebrows creased when I kissed his temple, swallowing the pang of guilt for the attention he'd lost. I went to Jack's side of the bed, fluffing his Minecraft comforter over him. His eye lids were swollen and almost translucent in the dark. Despite the slight frown, his face was serene. He was back for now. But for how long? Where were these episodes coming from and what were they doing to his developing brain? More importantly, what could we do? *What was wrong?*

One thing was undeniable; if I didn't know how to help my son, I had to find someone who did. In the silence of my sleeping house, I hopped online.

That was where I found Dr. Kovacevic. He was only a thirty-minute drive from our house, but it appeared most of his patients came from out of state. He was one of the few specialists treating kids with mysterious, sudden onset psychiatric illnesses. That little spark of hope ignited as I clung to his success rate and devoured testimonials. There were countless other parents and children out there suffering just like us. Why weren't people shouting from the rooftops? Why had so many doctors shrugged away my concerns? The flame of hope threatened to extinguish as I read further. Dr Kovacevic had a plethora of clients, suffering families lining up to see him. You couldn't even call for an appointment until he agreed to take your case via email. I squinted my tired eyes at the requirements.

Dr. Kovacevic asked for an email journal detailing symptom patterns from the onset. For the millionth time, I wished I'd pulled my head above water long enough to keep a journal. Still. I knew the kidnapper had first arrived around his third birthday. By now I recognized we could predict the abductor's arrival within a week of recovery from an illness. I remembered the rages.

Late into the night I wrote. I documented that night's rage and countless others. I shared the overnight transformation of our sweet, sensitive, easygoing, compliant child into a raging, angry, defiant three-year-old. Just as Jack had begged me to help him, I begged this doctor to help my son. Yes, begged. It seemed he was our last hope.

I couldn't sleep, instead spending time online, searching for answers. Finally, I dropped down to my knees at the side of my queen bed much like I had shortly before Jack was conceived. God had the answers. He would show me the way. Once again, I implored God to the soundtrack of the dogs breathing deeply, punctuated by Luke's soft snoring.

"God, Jack asked me for help. He's my child, but I don't know how to help him. He's Your child first. Tell me how to help him. Tell me what to do."

I said the last part with my eyes squeezed tightly shut. The ping of my phone on the nightstand interrupted my prayer. Instinctively I reached for it, seeing the email icon pop up on the illuminated screen. It was late at night. It had to be some useless, automated email wanting me to sign up for Instacart. I swiped at the screen and clicked on the email. The sender was Miroslav Kovacevic, MD. Holding my breath, I read the answer.

"I would gladly evaluate your son if so desired. Please contact my secretary (best time to call, 9–1), and she will assist you."

5

⸙

THE ANGEL IN A
WHITE LAB COAT

I pray that the eyes of your hearts may be enlightened in order
that you may know the hope to which He has called you…
—Ephesians 1:18

October 31, 2018

Dr. Kovacevic was slight man with tousled white hair, smart-looking
glasses, a melodic Croatian accent, and an inviting smile. He exuded
confidence. Jack's eyebrows were knit together, his expressive face
regarding the doctor with suspicion. I marched into that office filled
with anxious anticipation. He was one of the few specialists dealing
with Jack's set of symptoms. He was an answer to prayers.

His waiting room was typical doctor beige. We didn't have a
chance to sit before the friendly receptionist with light brown hair
and a wide smile showed us into the inner office. The room was the
size of a large closet. It contained a white porcelain sink and a black
stool aside a gray counter. Beige cabinets hung above the counter
with various barbies and action figures perched on top. On the other
side of the room was an examination table and two chairs crammed
between it and the door. Jack sat rigid in the chair closest to the door,
making himself as small as possible. I took the seat next to him.

Dr. Kovacevic blew into the room wearing a white lab coat over jeans and a faded blue button down. He told us to call him Dr. K.

"Hello, Mary Lue," he said to Jack. "Do you like Barbies? Which one up there would you like to take home?"

Jack glared at me, his eyes threatening to pop out of his head. I just smiled. Reviews and testimonials from other parents described Dr. K as eccentric and incredibly smart. His antics, questions, and curve balls were all a part of his assessment. He was not only bringing a little humor to a scary situation for the parents, but he was also noting the reactions of the child.

"I'm a boy," Jack said in a tone dripping with defiance. "I *hate* Barbies!"

Dr. K nodded sagely, making a note on his notepad. "Okay, Mary Lue, hop up on the table." He rolled his stool over and tapped the table with his ballpoint pen.

Jack glared at me again, his expression clearly saying, "Why did you bring me to see this guy?"

I strived to use openness and honesty with the kids. We'd discussed how this doctor helped kids who struggled, sometimes feeling out of control and acting in ways they wished they wouldn't. He assessed kids who were often sad and anxious, especially when separating or going to school. Dr. K would help us detect the cause and find a solution.

"I'm not going to public school," Jack had announced on the drive to the office. "If he says to put me in school, I'm not going."

"It's not about that, Jack." I glanced in the rearview mirror at him plastered against the seat, arms crossed. "We want to help you. You want to feel better, right?"

"Yeah," he'd answered in a soft voice.

Now Jack was watching Dr. K approach like he was the kid in the sandbox known for swiping toys. Dr. K asked Jack a few more questions and looked in his throat, ears, and nose. "Well," he said, looking at me over the top of his glasses. "First thing, he needs his tonsils and adenoids out."

I nodded. Jack had spent the last several years struggling on and off with seasonal allergies. Regular visits to the chiropractor and over the counter allergy medications helped. Allergy testing and mold inspections at our home came up negative. Still, I'd wondered about Jack's tonsils and adenoids. He often struggled to blow or breathe through his nose and went through periods of waking up congested and coughing and sneezing throughout the morning. Yet two separate ear, nose, and throat specialists had assured me his tonsils and adenoids looked only slightly enlarged and did not need to be removed. I explained this to Dr. K.

He nodded, making a *tsk, tsk* sound under his breath. "I work closely with Dr. Mahoney. She's a pediatric ENT. I'll send you to her." He spun his chair and rolled back to his counter. He scrawled a name and number on a yellow Post-It note and handed it to me. I looked down and copied the information into my notebook, knowing I'd likely lose the Post-It note before leaving the office. Fortunately, the ENT was in the same area as Dr. K.

"She books up fast. Call right away," Dr. K told me.

I handed him the clipboard of papers I'd brought—Jack's psychological evaluations and writing samples.

Dr. K pushed his glasses up and studied the pages, nodding to himself. "I'll have Diane make a copy of these." He turned to Jack. "I'm going to have you sit up front with Diane and help her with something, if that's okay with Mom. Can you draw her a house and a person?"

Jack shrugged. "Okay."

The doctor poked his head out the door. "Diane, Jack is going to sit with you and help you draw that house and person while I talk to Mom."

"Sure! Come on out here with me, Jack! Do you like suckers?" Diane's cheerful voice carried down the short hallway.

Jack looked at me, and I nodded encouragement, wondering if he'd go.

"After that, time to go home. No screaming, crying, or saying, 'I want to stay with Dr. K forever,' okay?"

My literal boy stopped just short of displaying his lack of appreciation for the doctor's humor with an eye roll. I watched him assess his options, ultimately following Diane out of the room. Dr. K closed the office door behind Jack and returned to his stool, spinning toward me, his demeanor suddenly serious.

"I do that for two reasons." He held up two long fingers. "The drawing of the house and the person tells me about what's going on neurologically." He tapped his temple with the pen. "Two, I don't like to talk too much in front of the kids. I keep it light with them."

I nodded, picking at my cuticles in my lap. "I appreciate that. I'm actually surprised he's out there with her. He struggles to separate from me."

"Yes, that's common," Dr. K said, almost to himself.

Common to what? I wondered.

"When did the separation anxiety begin?"

His phrasing of the question surprised me. Most people, doctors and counselors included, assumed Jack's separation anxiety went back to day one. I'd been not so subtly blamed for his anxious, insecure demeanor. Over the years, I'd accepted this blame. But I knew what they didn't; Jack didn't have an anxious and insecure demeanor. Not when he wasn't with the kidnapper.

"The separation anxiety started right when he turned three," I told Dr. K. "Before that, he went to park district programs and occasionally stayed with sitters with no problem. Well, I mean, when he was around eighteen months old, he went through a phase where he'd cry briefly when I left, but nothing like what popped up when he was three."

I peeked up at the doctor, bracing myself for the judgement. I waited for him to tell me maybe I needed to stop projecting my own worry onto my child, and I just needed to toughen up and get him used to me leaving. Maybe since I was a stay-at-home mom, I was around *too much*?

Dr. K studied me, his expression one of interest rather than judgement, his blue eyes slightly wide. "So he went through a phase of separation anxiety at eighteen months, which is developmentally appropriate, but then had no further difficulty with separation until he was three?"

"That's correct. We thought it was a phase or maybe a reaction to transition from an only child to a big brother, but—"

"It was much more severe and pervasive than previous separation anxiety, the duration was indefinite, and the onset was seemingly overnight?"

I nodded stupidly, probably resembling a bobblehead. "Yes. Yes, exactly! You've seen this before?"

"My dear, countless times." He regarded me thoughtfully. "Do you know what word in your email made me sure about taking your son's case?"

"What's that?"

"You likened the onset of Jack's symptoms to an abduction. With children I see, they're completely healthy Tuesday night, and very psychiatrically ill Wednesday morning."

I swallowed hard, firmly gripping my composure. *He's not waving me off. He's not telling me I'm crazy. He's not blaming me. He* believes *me.* A kidnapper had been pursuing my child and terrorizing my family for over six years, and Dr. K was the first professional to believe me. There's no adequate description for the relief of simply being believed.

"His entire personality changed overnight, right around his third birthday. Even his eyes look different when he's in a flare, his pupils are very dilated. If I didn't know better, I'd think it was demon possession. He develops tics too. Throat clearing, tongue clicking, and pacing."

Dr. K nodded, breaking eye contact only long enough to scratch a few notes on his pad.

"I gave you both of Jack's formal psych evals. He was diagnosed with high functioning autism at six, but a follow-up evaluation by a different clinician two years later did not detect autism but did detect persistent depressive disorder and generalized anxiety disorder. His counselor sees some signs of OCD, but again, the symptoms aren't consistent. Through the summer up until now it has seemed like one continual flare. But he's gone for weeks or months without symptoms."

Dr. K rummaged through the papers I'd given him, shaking out the stapled sheets documenting Jack's autism diagnosis. "I can understand why he was diagnosed with autism. These kids, they can present as autistic. But autism isn't there Tuesday and gone Thursday and then back again next week." He looked up at me. "I'd bet my medical license there's nothing autistic about your son."

I digested this new information. TJ had been diagnosed with moderate autism at three, three years prior. I'd begun to question Jack's diagnosis. He did have some hallmark traits of autism, like extreme sensitivity to noise and smell, rigidity surrounding rules and routines, difficulty reading subtle social cues, and obsessive interests. I think we all have obsessive interests, but at six, Jack could talk all day about the process and importance of recycling. For a child otherwise very observant, it never occurred to him that his peers may not share his enthusiasm or enjoy being lectured about throwing their water bottle in the recycling so it wouldn't sit in a landfill for six million years.

While TJ had periods of ups and downs, we didn't see him completely transform. Though he could get aggressive and out of control during meltdowns, he could still be reasoned with and eventually calmed. He didn't go somewhere else the way Jack did. But if Jack wasn't on the spectrum, what was causing these flares? Even his anxiety and mood symptoms seemed to fluctuate. I was relieved I'd found someone to listen, but could Dr. K tell us how to release Jack from his abductor, the invisible force that held our family hostage, forcing us to live in helpless fear and confusion during bad times and hypervigilance in times of calm?

Dr. K put the papers down, picked up his notebook and pen, and looked at me. "Why don't you start at the beginning?"

6

A THIEF IN THE NIGHT

Shall I accept good from the hand of the Lord, but not evil?

—Job 42:6–7

May 2012

It was a muggy night in late May. I was newly pregnant, nauseous, and exhausted. Luke was out of town for work. Jack had gone to sleep peacefully hours earlier. Just like every night, I crept into Jack's room before I went to bed myself, checked on him, and tucked him in. We had a pretty solid routine, heading upstairs for bath and bed-time preparations and books, and lights out by seven forty-two. For some reason, that probably has a scientific basis, pregnancy always brought out the obsessive in me. Anyway, Jack's compliant behavior and our routine would ease us into life with a newborn.

When I leaned down to kiss Jack's sweet head, heat rose up to meet me. I frowned. He'd been completely fine all day, not even a sniffle. His mood had been characteristically sunny.

I dashed across the hall to the bathroom and rummaged in the messy drawers, overly stuffed with random bath toys, extra tubes of toothpaste, and dental floss. Locating the temporal thermometer behind some bath crayons, I returned to my almost three-year-old's room and pressed the thermometer to his temple. The corners of Jack's closed eyes crinkled in a frown, but he remained asleep. His long lashes brushed his cheek. The thermometer beeped. I raised it to my eyes and squinted in the dim light offered by the nightlight: 103.4.

My eyes widened. I took his temperature again, pressing the back of my hand to his sweaty forehead. The temperature was accurate. Just a few hours prior, Jack had gone to sleep with a hug, a kiss, and a tuck. "Night, Mommy. I love you." He'd prayed for Dad to have a safe trip home the next day. But he hadn't complained of a single symptom, and he'd been cool. Whatever this was had snuck in since he'd gone to sleep.

I typically tried to avoid medicating fevers, subscribing to the theory of letting a virus run its course. But Jack had never had a fever this high before. *At what temperature are kids at risk for febrile seizures?* I wondered. I raced downstairs and grabbed the children's Tylenol from the high shelf of a kitchen cabinet. Carefully, I filled the small plastic measuring cup and returned to Jack's room. He looked so peaceful; I hated to wake him.

"Jack." I gently shook his shoulder. "Jack, hunny, wake up for a minute. Do you feel okay?"

He mumbled and rolled over.

"Jack." I rolled him back over. "You have a little fever. Mommy's going to give you some medicine."

Jack's eyes fluttered open. The blue was hazy with sleep. "Am I okay, Mommy?"

"You'll be okay. I'm just going to give you a little medicine." I helped him swallow the clear liquid and gave him a drink from his sippy cup on his dresser. "How do you feel?"

"Okay. Tired."

"Okay. Go back to sleep. I'll come check on you again in a little bit."

"Okay, Mommy. Love you."

"Love you too, Bean."

"Mommy?"

"Yes, sweetie?"

"I'm cold."

"Okay."

I covered him with a light blanket. His eyes were already closing. Suddenly wide awake, I crossed back to the bathroom and turned on the tap, waiting for the water in the old pipes to reach a tepid temperature. Reaching into the bottom drawer, I retrieved a white washcloth adorned with cheerful yellow ducks, held it under the stream, and wrung it out. By the time I returned to his room, Jack was already asleep. I felt his head and took his temperature again, as though expecting a change in the last several minutes. Then again, why wouldn't I? This fever had appeared spontaneously.

After thoroughly washing my hands and wiping every surface with disinfectant wipes, I checked on Jack again. His skin had cooled slightly. I washed my hands again. At not quite twelve weeks pregnant, extra caution was warranted around germs. With a two-year-old, this was no small undertaking.

Back in my own bed, I turned HGTV on low and set my alarm for two hours later so I could take Jack's temperature again. I fell asleep thinking of Jack's Big Brother shirt. We planned on him wearing it when our family came to our house for his third birthday party ten days away. I'd be just over twelve weeks. My mom and in-laws already knew, but I couldn't wait to see the reactions of my aunts, uncles, and cousins. (Spoiler: Most of them already suspected.)

I checked on Jack every two hours throughout the night. His temperature went down, though never reached normal. The following morning, he slept until almost eight—a rarity. His temperature was around 101. Still, he showed no symptoms other than a slight runny nose and lethargy. I watched the second hand drag itself around the clock until 9:00 AM. The automated message of the pediatrician's office droned in my ear as I wrapped my fingers on the cheap green Formica countertops. After a quick explanation of Jack's symptoms and information of my pregnancy, the doctor agreed to see Jack that morning.

"What'd the doctor say?" My mom, Margaret, who'd spent the night, wrung her hands at the kitchen table.

I turned to her. "They said to bring him in at ten thirty."

"Did you tell them you're pregnant?"

"Yes," I responded, even though she'd heard my end of the conversation. "Jack, would you like some breakfast? Cookie Monster waffles? Cheerios?"

Jack flopped onto the couch with his snuggle blankie, a tattered, well-loved white cloth adorned with pirates. For some reason, he'd latched on to that one blanket from the collection as a baby. He stuck his thumb in his mouth, a habit he'd abandoned months before. "Can I watch Clifford?"

"Sure." I flipped on the TV and found the latest on demand Clifford episode.

Hi! I'm Emily Elizabeth, and this is Clifford, my big red dog.

The sing-song voice comforted Jack but grated on my nerves, the cheer conspicuously highlighting my plummeting mood. Remember how anxious I'd been while carrying Jack? Well, my concerns hadn't diminished with a second pregnancy, as I'd hoped. I was worried about Jack, looking so lifeless on the couch. I was worried about Luke flying home from New York. I was worried about my not quite twelve-week pregnancy. I was even worried about my worrying; it couldn't be good for the baby.

"Jack, hunny bunny, do you want Gramma Margaret to make you breakfast?"

"Not now. I'm not hungry," he mumbled from under the throw blanket.

"At least toast, hunny?" my mom persisted.

"No, thanks."

"Drink some water for now." I brought him a small plastic cup of cool water, holding the straw to his dry lips.

"Fluid is very important," my mom said almost to herself. "Hope, it's unlike him to not want breakfast, and to be so tired in the morning."

"He's sick, Mom." I shrugged with false calm. "Probably just a virus. We'll see what the doctor says."

"A virus." Dr. Confidence nodded at me, pushing his swivel stool back from the examination table with more force than necessary. He deftly deposited his latex gloves and a thin wooden tongue depressor into the garbage. "His ears look good. Throat looks good, only slightly red. His lungs are completely clear."

"So no pneumonia, Doctor?" my mom asked.

"None whatsoever."

"What about a strep test?" I asked. "Shouldn't we rule that out?"

Dr. Confidence shook his head. "No need. His throat might be a little irritated from the postnasal drip, but it doesn't look super red or inflamed. All you can do is push fluids, lots of rest, and let in run its course."

"Doctor, Hope is eleven weeks pregnant. Could this harm the baby?"

Dr. Confidence ran a hand through his thick brown hair, removing a pen form his shirt pocket and clicking it absently. "Not likely. However, roseola is going around. If that's what it is, he'll have a fever for several days. When the fever breaks, he'll get a red splotchy rash on his torso. Again, it's viral, so just watch it. Practice diligent hand washing. Call your OBGYN if you're concerned." As if he needed to tell me.

My OBGYN echoed Dr. Confidence's advice on diligent hand washing and assured me that I'd likely been exposed to roseola at some point and developed immunity. "Keep taking your prenatal vitamins!" the nurse crowed in a voice several octaves higher than when she'd answered the phone. *"It was that paranoid mom again,"* I pictured her telling her coworkers after ending the call. *"Yeah, the Google addict calling about every possible scenario."*

Jack's fever fluctuated over the next week, but never reached as high as that first night. His symptoms remained nonspecific and never advanced past a slight runny nose, mild diarrhea, and a persistent fever. Luke came home, and I focused on caring for a sick toddler, hand washing, and cleaning.

"I hope we don't have to cancel his party," I told Luke. "He's been so excited. Our big three-year-old."

"I'm excited too. For Jack, and for our new baby," he answered, placing his hand on my tiny bump.

"I just hope we don't have to cancel," I repeated.

"I'm sure he'll be fine, Hope. You've been taking great care of him."

That was my Luke. His unwavering confidence that everything would be fine made me believe it too.

On day six, the fever broke. Jack was up and running, his usual playful self. I breathed a huge sigh of relief, disinfected the house again, and started blowing up balloons.

The relief was short-lived, however. I didn't know, couldn't know, that the kidnapper was lurking just outside our windows, watching the yellow, green, red, and blue balloons floating around our son's feet and above his head as he threw them up and giggled when they floated gently to the ground.

Two days later, eight days after the onset of Jack's fever, the symptoms—the high fever, runny nose, and lethargy reappeared just as suddenly. He never did get the rash. More confused than ever, I called the pediatrician's office and explained the curious trajectory of Jack's symptoms. He'd been symptom-free for two days, but the high fever was back.

"Let me put you on a brief hold," the nurse said.

I paced the front room and stared out the picture window at the beautiful spring day. It felt like an eternity before the nurse returned to the line.

"Mrs. Shepherd? I spoke to Dr. Confidence. He wants you to take your son to Golden's emergency room for testing."

7

NO EXPLANATION

*Listen to my words, oh Lord, consider my lament. Hear my
cry for help, my King and my God, for to you I pray.*
—Psalm 5:1–2

May 2012

My stomach rolled as I filled a sippy cup with half water and half
apple juice. *Not now*, I thought, shoving some saltines in my mouth
on my trip through the kitchen. I'd called my mom and Luke. Both
agreed to meet us at the hospital. My mom had a plethora of questions that I couldn't answer. Why did they want us to go to the emergency room? Was it just to rule out something serious? What exactly
were they testing for? What did it mean that the fever had gone away
for two days and then returned? Was it a virus? Infection? *What was
wrong?*

I gathered snuggle blankie and stuffed monkey. "Jack, Dr.
Confidence wants us to take you to the hospital for a few tests," I
said brightly, as though I'd announced a simple errand.

Jack's blue eyes peered up at me from the couch. "Will it hurt?
Will I have to get a shot?"

The familiar gut-wrenching desire to take the pain of your child
upon yourself settled over me. They'd need to draw blood, which
Jack hadn't had done before. "You might have to get a little poke,

hunny. But Mommy, Daddy, and Grandma will be there. It'll be really quick, and I'll hold your hand the whole time."

Jack began to cry soft, weak, heartbreaking tears. "It will hurt. It's not fair."

"I know, Bean. I'd do it for you if I could."

"But why?"

"We just have to make sure your virus is going away so you can get better as soon as possible." *And make sure it's nothing worse than a virus.*

As I carried Jack, snuggle blankie, and monkey to the car with my tote bag slug over my shoulder, I thought of all the parents sitting in hospital rooms waiting, suffering along with their children. My heart ached for the parents who had to watch their children struggle with illness on a regular basis.

Jack was quiet for the ten-minute drive to the hospital. Fortunately, I snagged a spot in the ER parking lot, ignoring the maze of the general parking garage. I balanced Jack on my hip, his head hot and clammy on my shoulder. Shuffling past several people slumped in green upholstered chairs in the waiting room, I gave the smiling nurse at the registration desk our names and informed her that Dr. Confidence had sent us.

"Sure, we'll get you right back. Let me see your wrist, sweetie."

Always my compliant boy, Jack shifted monkey to his other hand and stiffly held out a wrist. Luckily the pediatric portion of the ER did not have a waiting room; children were taken back immediately. After inputting our information, the nurse led us through a thick sliding glass door, down a hallway, past a nurse's station, and down another hallway, finally stopping at a glassed-in cubicle. I tried to keep up, irrationally resenting the chatting nurses and laughing paramedics. For them, this was just another day. I longed for just another day.

The nurse slid a heavy Plexiglas door and a beige curtain open. "You can go ahead and help him change into that gown." She nodded toward the white gown with blue polka dots folded neatly at the foot of the gurney. "Dr. Nonchalant will be right with you."

"When will I get the shot?" Jack spoke for the first time since leaving home.

The nurse smiled sympathetically. "Oh, hunny, the doctor will take good care of you," she said, expertly evading Jack's question. "I'll give you some privacy." She offered me one more smile of sympathy and exited, pulling the curtain but leaving the sliding door ajar.

I sat Jack on the gurney and worked his shirt over his head. He instantly wrapped his spindly arms around his skinny torso. "I'm cold, Mommy."

"Here, let's put this on quickly, and we can get you under the blanket." I tied the gown and pulled back the scratchy white blanket, pulling it up to Jack's chin. His eyes slid over to the small flat screen TV suspended on an arm in the center of the room.

"Want to watch a show?"

Jack nodded. I flipped through the meager channels, landing on a cartoon asking viewers to help fill in the words of nursery rhymes. I couldn't remember the name of the show, but I was glad for the distraction.

"Oh, this room? Thank you so much. Yes, my grandson. Who's the doctor today? Is he experienced?" My mom's gregarious voice bounced into the room.

"Here's Grandma!" The nurse moved aside the curtain. She gave me a worried look and retreated.

"Hi, Jack, hunny, Grandma's here. How're you feeling?"

Jack peeked up at her. "Not so good."

"Aw, poor fish." My mom turned and hugged me. "What did they say? Has the doctor been in yet?"

"Not yet," I replied, offering a chair to my mom.

I'd barely dropped into the blue plastic chair next to Jack's head when a young woman in black scrubs rolled a computer into the room. "Registration," she announced curtly.

I again handed over my license and insurance card, answering repetitive questions. "Do you feel safe in your home?" she asked robotically.

"Yes," I answered in the same tone, wondering why they couldn't simply refer to whatever had been filled out upon our arrival.

Do you feel safe in your home? I understood and appreciated the necessity of the question, but at the time, it was irrelevant to me personally. Home was my safe place. I couldn't predict a future in which I wouldn't feel safe there.

"Will the doctor be in soon, miss?" my mom asked, wringing her hands.

Her heavily lined eyes cut over to my mom. "I don't know, ma'am. I'm just registration."

I wondered idly whether her legal name was registration or if she'd been at the job so long she'd forfeited her identity. It was easier than wondering about what the blood tests would reveal.

If you've been to the ER, you know whether you're escorted directly back or not, no matter how old or young or sick you are, there's a lot of waiting. At some point, Luke arrived. We exchanged worried looks over Jack's bed. One show turned into another. My mom paced, went outside to smoke, and asked anyone in scrubs when the doctor would be in. I'm not sure how much time passed when the doctor, a slight Asian man wearing a white lab coat over powder blue scrubs came in. The show immediately lost Jack's attention. He began to cry.

"No, I don't want a shot!" He hid his arms under the thin blanket and scooted closer to me.

I rubbed his head. "I know, sweetie. It'll be quick."

It wasn't. Dr. Nonchalant wrote down Jack's symptoms.

"What does it sound like, Doctor?" my mom asked from her seat by the wall.

"Well, several viruses are going around, although the fever subsiding and returning a couple days later is curious." He tugged at the stethoscope hanging around his neck. "I'll know more after I get the bloodwork back. Hang tight."

He made his exit as two nurses entered with vials, a syringe, Band-Aids, and stickers. Stickers would never be enough to make a needle more palatable.

Jack squeezed his eyes shut and wailed while the nurse tried to find a vein. Luke and I held Jack's hands and spoke soothing words through his cries. Finally, it was over. I lowered the bar and scooted in next to Jack, holding him close, my concern over catching something taking a back seat.

"Where's snuggle blankie?" Jack sniffed. Luke disentangled it from the twisted blanket. We waited.

At some point, my mom made a trip to the vending machine for pretzels and chips. She vacillated between offering each of us food and pacing the halls asking if anyone had seen the doctor.

Eventually, Dr. Nonchalant bustled back in, his eyes sweeping over us before returning to the clipboard in his hand. "Well, his white cell count was slightly elevated," he said to the clipboard.

"What does that indicate?" I asked, the way someone asks a question when they're not sure they want the answer.

"Well, it indicates the body is fighting something. Could be several things…"

He said a bunch of other words, one of which was "leukemia." My mom gasped.

"But his symptoms are still consistent with a virus. It's more likely a virus."

Once the "L" word was out there it remained suspended, polluting the already germ-laden air. I kissed Jack's clammy head as the doctor left in pursuit of more test results.

No one said anything much after that. Time became a vacuum, too fast and too slow, ceasing to exist. Even my mom was quiet, intermittently holding out a bag of pretzels to me. I shook my head, my stomach knotted. My heart went out in silent solidarity to every parent in every hospital room waiting for a verdict.

We were blessed. The remainder of Jack's bloodwork looked normal. "So why is his white cell count elevated?" I asked.

Dr. Nonchalant just caught himself from shrugging. "His body is fighting something. A virus. Take extra precaution with hand washing, being pregnant."

"What about a strep test?" I persisted. Of course, I was beyond relieved nothing serious had shown up, but we were left with no answers.

Dr. Nonchalant shook his head. "Not necessary. I don't see many positive strep tests in kids his age. His throat is just a little red, but that's to be expected with the postnasal drip."

"Doctor," Luke interjected, "we have family coming over this weekend for Jack's birthday party. Should we cancel?"

I sighed, having forgotten all about the party.

"You may have to, it depends," Dr. Nonchalant said. "If he's fever- and symptom-free for twenty-four hours, you can go ahead with it."

"I don't wanna cancel my party!" Jack wailed. It was the first he'd spoken in the last half hour. I smiled, relieved he had enough stamina to worry about his party.

"Just drink lots of fluids and rest, buddy. Happy birthday," Dr. Nonchalant said on the way out.

"Can we go home now?" Jack's sweet blue eyes peered up at me.

I brushed Jack's thick brown hair out of his eyes. "Yep, let's go home."

I made a mental note to throw snuggle blankie, monkey, and all of our clothes directly into the wash machine once we arrived home. We gathered our things, and Luke carried Jack out to the parking lot.

"See you at home, buddy." Luke transferred Jack to me, and I settled him in the Santa Fe while Luke retreated to his smaller Alero.

"Bye, Jack. Gram loves you. Remember what the doctor said and drink lots of water." My mom leaned into the back seat and kissed Jack's head. She straightened up and gripped my arm. "Will you call me and let me know how he is?"

"Of course."

"I was worried when the doctor said 'leukemia,'" she whispered.

"I know. Me too. But it's just a virus."

We went home. Within the next two days, Jack's symptoms disappeared. That weekend my aunts, uncles, and cousins, my mom, and Luke's parents as well as a few friends gathered at our house to celebrate Jack's third birthday. Jack dashed to the door each time the bell rang and proudly displayed his Big Brother T-shirt.

Luke's mom, Loraine, and Jack went exploring in the yard, coming back into the house with a long, slimy earth worm. The two conspirators watched me for my reaction. I acted grossed out when my three-year-old put the cold, wriggly worm in my palm, but I was savoring every moment. I was savoring having a healthy child, glad the mysterious virus had come to an end.

Little did I know that virus was only the beginning.

8

JUST A PHASE

But I did not believe these things until I
came and saw with my own eyes.

—1 Kings 10

Summer 2012

The fall of 2012 was a season of change. Our lives transformed insidiously along with the color of the leaves. My pregnancy progressed as expected. We found out we were having a boy. Jack was thrilled to find out he was getting a brother, though I think he envisioned an instant playmate rather than a strange infant who only cried, slept, and pooped. Jack would say as much after TJ's birth. We took Jack to a "big siblings" class at the hospital. We sat at a long table with a handful of other expectant couples while a smattering of young children sat in a circle in front of the table learning to hold and feed a doll. We took a ridiculous number of pictures and hung Jack's Official Big Brother certificate on his bedroom wall.

I couldn't wait to meet the baby. Just as I had throughout my pregnancy with Jack, I constantly envisioned this little person. Who would he be? Would he love Clifford like Jack? Would he be an animal lover, a sports fan, a math whiz? What habit of his would drive me crazy? What cute words would come out of his mouth? It always cracked me up when people said, "Oh, wow, your pregnancy is going by so fast!" *To whom?* I'd wonder. For me, it may as well have been a decade. I was anxious to hold the baby, but I was also looking forward to not being pregnant. You know those women who love pregnancy and positively glow? Yeah, that wasn't me.

With TJ, I was almost constantly nauseous for the duration of the pregnancy. Jack loved to go on weekly "garbage walks." Every week on garbage day we'd walk around the neighborhood so Jack could close people's cans and roll them up their driveway. He earned a reputation as being quite the helper. I came to enjoy this routine with Jack. During my pregnancy, however, I'd attempt to hold my breath as long as possible to avoid the smell of garbage, accentuated by my pregnancy nose.

The changes in Jack following his third birthday that summer were more pronounced than the changes taking place in my body. We were fortunate to have access to an active park district with a variety of classes and programs for everyone from infants to seniors. Jack and I had started participation in a baby gymnastics class before he was even crawling. Insert first-kid jokes here. Jack and I both looked forward to these scheduled activities. When he turned two, Jack was able to proudly enter the class by himself while the parents waited in the stuffy hallway.

"Your son is so easygoing," the other parents would comment as they observed Jack march confidently into the class and come out with a smile and a hug, proudly thrusting a craft usually including macaroni into my lap.

Jack had a secure attachment. He was so proud to go into his "big boy" classes. If I'm being honest, as much as I enjoyed doing the classes with Jack, I didn't hate having thirty minutes to sit in the hallway and read or chat with other parents.

The summer he turned three, I took him to a Sports of Sorts class. The class featured a preschool version of one sport each week for four weeks. Since infanthood we'd been exposing Jack to various activities so he could explore his interests. This would give him a chance to try out soccer, T-ball, floor hockey, and basketball. We'd signed up for the class months before, and Jack had been looking forward to it.

I brought him to The Barn—an actual barn converted into a park district building. We waited in the hallway for the half door to the large arena to open. I held Jack up so he could see into the arena. Plastic hockey sticks waited. The teenage girl opened the door and the children filed in. That's when the unexpected happened. Jack turned from the door and threw his arms around my legs. Misinterpreting his gesture, I hugged him. "Have a good class, Jack. Mommy will be right out here."

"No!" he wailed, attempting to wrap his legs around me. We received a few sideways glances from parents exiting the class sans children.

I struggled to squat down to Jack's level. "What's wrong, bean? You've been excited about this class, remember? It looks like you're going to play hockey today. You get to hit a little puck with those sticks." (This is the extent of my sports knowledge, by the way.)

"No! I want you to go in with me!"

"Jack, this is just for big kids, remember? I can watch you from the doorway. Remember, Mommy waits outside, and I'm right here when you're done?"

"No!" Jack tightened his grip on me.

The teenager approached, messy blond ponytail bouncing, a smile just barely masking her annoyance. "Come on, buddy, it's time for class to start. We're going to have so much fun!"

"I'll walk you in," I told Jack. I took his hand and led him to the other kids lined up by the wall. "Okay, line up with these kids. You're going to play some games. See you in a few minutes." I tried to make a nonchalant exit to show Jack this was no big deal. I only made it a few steps before he launched himself at me, wailing like a siren. I caught a few looks of alarm from other kids.

I gave him a hug then attempted to hold him at arm's length. "Come on, sweetie, you've done this a ton of times now. You're going to have fun, and I'll be right there." I pointed to the door a mere six feet away.

"I don't want to! No, please, don't make me go!" Jack grew more hysterical.

"Has he taken a class by himself before?" The teenager's smile evaporated. I can't say I blamed her. I doubt she was being adequately compensated to deal with a screaming child.

"Yes," I answered over Jack's wailing. "He's done several. He just did Gym Tigers in the spring."

"Well, maybe you should come back next week. We can't really have him in here crying, ya know?"

I nodded, my face burning. She wasn't wrong. It obviously wasn't working this week. Besides, it was peewee sports, not training for the Olympics. "Okay, Jack, we'll go home and try again next week."

I hoisted Jack onto my hip and navigated through the hallway of waiting parents, some of whom looked down at phones while a few offered me sympathetic smiles.

"Sorry," the girl called after us.

Back in the car, Jack immediately stopped crying. I settled him in the car seat and studied his puffy eyes and red nose. I reached into the front seat where I'd left my diaper bag. Although Jack had been fully potty-trained for months, I still carried a sippy cup, snacks, a change of clothes, wipes, and hand sanitizer. I pulled a baby wipe from the package and wiped Jack's nose.

"What's wrong, Jack?"

"I'm hungry," he said.

"Okay." I sprayed some alcohol-free hand sanitizer into his hands and handed him a snack trap of Annie's cheddar bunnies. "But why didn't you want to stay at class? You usually love the park district classes. Were you nervous?'

Jack shrugged, yellow crumbs cascading down his Clifford shirt. "I just don't wanna do it."

"Okay, well, maybe next week?"

During the short drive home, I contemplated Jack's sudden refusal to do the class. It wasn't a big deal, I reasoned. Except his behavior was so out of the ordinary. He hadn't shown an ounce of separation anxiety since he was eighteen months old, and even then, it consisted of a few weak protests at being left, with him calming down right away. Maybe he was tired? He'd begun to give up his naps. I glanced at the clock on the dash. It was only 9:45 AM.

Once home, I tried to lay in Jack's bed with him. We read some books, and I sang "You Are My Sunshine" to him. He never did fall asleep. Eventually we got up and did puzzles and then met some friends at the park. Jack was his usually cheerful self the rest of the day, and I shrugged off the failed class. He was being a fickle three-year-old.

The following week we returned to the class. "Do you want to go to Sports of Sorts today?" I asked Jack before leaving the house.

"Yeah," he answered. "Why wouldn't I?"

I shrugged. *Didn't he remember?* "Just asking." I slung the tote bag over my shoulder, and we were off.

We parked in the parking lot and Jack took my hand. On the sidewalk outside The Barn door, Jack squatted to study an army of ants marching across the path. I snuck a peek at the time on my phone, trying not to hurry him. He smiled up at me. Hand in hand, we went in.

Jack walked along beside me into the building, down the hallway, all the way to the arena doorway. The kids were filing in. Jack stopped dead at the door.

"Okay, Jack, have fun! Mommy will be right out here," I said brightly.

Jack spun around in the doorway. A little boy ducked under his arm and darted into the class. "I want you to come in with me." Jack's eyes began to water.

My heart dropped. "I'll walk you in, and then I'm going to wait in the hallway with the other parents." Shaking off the deja vu, I led Jack through the door to the far wall where kids were lining up behind a blue plastic T and a yellow plastic bat. The teenage girl tugged on a blond pigtail and threw me a worried look.

"Wow, T-ball today! Looks like fun. I'll be right out th—"

Jack hurled himself at my leg, latching on like a barnacle. "Noo! I don't want to! I want you to stay!"

"Jack, what's wrong?" The other kids openly gaped. My face burned as I tried to extricate Jack from my leg.

"I want to go home!" Jack shrieked.

"Ma'am," the teenager said in a scolding tone, "he may not be ready for this class. He has to be able to do it without you. If we let you stay, then we have to let the other parents stay, and then it becomes a totally different class, see? Once they're three, we expect them to do the classes independently."

"He's been doing classes here independently," I said.

Jack let go of my leg and yanked on my arm. The teenager's eyes slid over to him. "This class is three to five-year-olds. Maybe sign up again next year, 'kay?" She turned her back to me and blew the silver whistle hanging around her neck.

Jack let out an unrecognizable scream and plastered his hands over his ears.

"What's wrong with that boy?" a child asked.

I lifted Jack, his hands firmly planted over his ears, my tote bag swinging precariously off my arm. An orange sippy cup with a blue lid dropped out of my bag and rolled as I hurried down the hallway. A grandpa took pity on me and retrieved it.

"Thank you," I said through gritted teeth as I shifted Jack so I could grab the cup.

"Hope your day gets better," he responded.

"Poor guy really doesn't want to be here," someone commented helpfully as I reached the door. I was sweating by the time we crossed the parking lot to the car. I buckled Jack into his car seat, sprayed alcohol-free sanitizer into his little palms and dove into the front seat. In the safety of my silver Santa Fe, I caught my breath and glanced at Jack in the rearview mirror. His eyes were red rimmed and puffy. He lifted his foot and bit the strap of his blue rubber sandal, something else I hadn't seen him do before.

"Hunny, don't put that in your mouth." I paused. "What's wrong?"

He looked at me with that expressive face of his, forehead creased. "What do you mean? Nothing."

"I'm surprised you didn't want to do the class, that's all. You said you wanted to. You always seem to enjoy park district activities. You've done so many classes by yourself."

He shrugged. "I don't like this class."

I frowned. He never expressed dislike of a park district class before. "But you haven't gone into this class. How do you know you don't like it?" I didn't care that much about the park district class. Looking back, I think I was desperate for a simple explanation for Jack's sudden separation anxiety and intolerance of the whistle.

"I just know, okay? I don't want to do it. All park district classes are boring and stupid!" Jack kicked the back of my seat.

"Jack! We don't say 'stupid.'"

"Sorry, Mommy. Can we go to the park?"

I sighed, contemplating the best way to navigate this new parenting terrain. If I took him to the park, was that rewarding him? But should I punish him for not wanting me to leave him? He was three, and it was a park district class. At the end of the day, it wasn't a big deal. I was so preoccupied with doing parenting "right"; I hadn't learned the right way to parent was filled with so many shades of gray.

I ended up taking him to the park. He made friends with another little boy. They played together in the sandbox. I sat on the edge, trying not to collect sand in my bag. My dark, pin-straight hair had fallen half out of my ponytail. A mom sporting braided auburn hair, a baby pink sundress, and matching jeweled flip flops came up alongside the sandbox rolling a Bugaboo stroller back and forth. "Five more minutes, Robert."

"I'm playin wit my friend." The boy pointed at Jack. "He likes Clifford."

I squinted up at the mom. Where had I put my sunglasses? I hoped they were at home. It was the third pair of cheap sunglasses I'd purchased that summer alone. "They made friends," I said unnecessarily. I cringed inwardly. I'm about as good at small talk as a politician is at humility.

She smiled down at me, the sunlight spilling around her. "So sweet. How old is your son?"

"He's three. How old are your kids?"

"Robert's three." He starts preschool this year. And Ava's six months." She nodded to the bundle in the stroller.

I nodded. "Our second is due in December."

"Oh!" she squealed. "Congratulations. Is your son excited to be a big brother?"

"I think so." I straightened up and lowered my voice. "But Jack's shown some separation anxiety. He's been completely over that for the last year and a half. Last week and this week, he refused to let me leave him at the park district programs."

She nodded. "That's normal. Robert went through that when I was pregnant with Ava. Their world is changing, and they don't know how to express it, you know? Besides, three's a tough age."

I nodded, relieved. Jack was losing his only child status. He was approaching preschool and exercising more independence—and attitude. Oh, the attitude. He'd developed it as the flames of the candles on his third birthday cake flickered out. My respectful, easygoing boy had begun back talking us and exhibiting outward defiance. Surely, this wasn't unusual; I'd heard similar accounts from other mothers.

Except, the phase didn't pass. Jack's defiant behavior escalated. Screaming, slamming, and locking his door (something he knew he wasn't supposed to do) and shockingly disrespectful talk became everyday events. Prior to that summer, I could count on one hand the number of times Jack had thrown a tantrum. He began to have extreme meltdowns, sometimes several times a day. These episodes could last anywhere from twenty minutes to several hours and looked much different from toddler tantrums.

The meltdowns escalated beyond screaming and crying. Jack would rip through the house like a tornado, tearing objects off shelves and hurling them like grenades. The first time Jack had one of these episodes I remember thinking it resembled a possession. His eyes were empty, like he was somewhere else.

We tried time-outs. Each time-out became a ridiculous game in which Jack vacated the time-out chair and ran around laughing and knocking things over, and Luke or me walking him back to the chair and resetting the three-minute timer. And repeat. We tried sitting with him in his room, holding him or reading to him until he calmed down. Oftentimes, Luke had to hold him in his room so he wouldn't hurt himself or us or destroy anything.

These episodes could be triggered by nothing, and they passed as suddenly as they came. A literal switch seemed to flip as light flooded back into his eyes. He seemed disoriented and exhausted, apologizing tearfully.

Jack developed repetitive mannerisms. He'd constantly clear his throat, click his tongue, and walk-skip back and forth. Always articulate beyond his age, Jack periodically transitioned to "baby talk" or a "robot voice." We consulted an ear-nose-and throat doctor, who chalked the throat clearing up to seasonal allergies. We consulted our pediatrician. He assured us Jack was going through a phase, possibly a growth spurt.

"Nothing is wrong with my son," Luke declared regularly.

"He's never been like this before," I protested. "When I go to the bathroom, he sticks his hands under the door and cries. He panics if I go into a separate room. And his behavior—it's completely unlike him."

"He's three. I think it's all to be expected, like the doctor said. Think about it from a three-year-old's point of view. I've been travelling more. We have a new baby coming. He's starting preschool. You haven't been feeling well throughout the pregnancy. That's a lot of change for an adult, let alone a three-year-old."

"Maybe you're right." Everything he said made sense. "I hope you're right. But it's such a drastic change. He's different. I can't shake the feeling that something's off."

Luke threw up his hands. "Hope, I love you, but sometimes you go looking for something to go wrong. The doctor told you. Other parents have told you. He's fine. It's a phase. You'll see. Nothing is wrong with him."

He's right, I told myself. *Jack's fine. Everything's fine. It's a phase Everyone's right. I'm worrying over nothing.*

I repeated these words over and over to myself like a mantra.

But I never fully believed them.

9

LIFE AS WE KNEW IT

"Be alert and of sober mind. Your enemy the devil prowls around like a roaring lion looking for someone to devour."
—1 Peter 5:8

September 2012

Jack's resistance to park district activities persisted. I had to remove him from several classes. Often, I couldn't even get him out of the car, his little fingers gripping the seatbelt like I was attempting to drag him into a beehive. Just when I was about to give up on classes and camps altogether, he'd surprise me again, enthusiastically taking on a class with barely a backward glance. This would go on, sometimes for weeks, before he'd revert back to screaming and clinging to me. I vacillated between trying to coax him or completely scraping the class to relieve his discomfort. Either way, I wrestled with guilt and uncertainty. I wasn't being consistent. Nothing was consistent, except the fact that everything had changed.

I approached the milestone of Jack's first day of preschool weighed down by concealed trepidation. After researching a few options and visiting a few schools, we decided on Good Shepherd Lutheran Preschool, a welcoming, casual, friendly environment whose staff oozed dedication and wore only smiles. My close friend Adalyn and I attended parent orientations together while our husbands stayed home with the kids. We went out for drinks afterward; Angry Orchard for her and club soda with lime for me, as I was pregnant. Adalyn and I had been friends for two years, since we'd met at a mom's group at our Catholic church, Saint Agnus. A mutual friend introduced us, and we hit it off during a summer zoo trip when Jack was only thirteen months old and barely walking. Her son, Owen was only nine months older than Jack. The boys became perfect playmates.

Adalyn is the best kind of person. At first, she's quiet and reserved. She doesn't trust you right away, but when you get to know her and earn her your trust, she's nothing short of a 3:00 AM friend. She's the friend everyone needs. Throughout the years, our children have bonded as much as she and I. With Adalyn, I could openly share my concerns with Jack's behavior and personality changes and my anxiety over him beginning preschool. She's the rare kind of person who will sit and listen without minimizing your worries. It was comforting to know we were in this starting preschool thing together. We'd already requested for Jack and Owen to be in the same class. We were confident this would help ease the transition for both boys.

With each failed summer park district class, my uncertainty expanded like a balloon in the mouth of an eager party host. The school was perfect. The director and teachers assured me repeatedly that my son would adjust and that the teachers were well versed in separation anxiety, though I doubted they expected more than first day jitters—easily redirected with unfamiliar toys.

"I'm sure being in with Owen will help, and the class is small. Only twelve kids," Adalyn said, tearing the label of her Angry Orchard.

I stirred the ice in my club soda. "Yeah, I think having Owen with him will definitely help." I paused. "It's just, he was so hysterical at the park district programs; well, he was hysterical at some of them. Others, he went in no problem. I don't know what to expect on the first day of preschool."

"He did okay at preview day, right?"

Preview day was a scheduled hour where half the class visited the classroom to play and do an art project with their parents or caregivers. "Yeah, he loved the toys, especially the garbage truck."

Adalyn smiled. "Of course."

"And he played with some of the other kids."

"He is social."

"But I was there. He's fine if I'm right there."

Adalyn nodded slowly, dragging a nacho through guacamole. "Well, Ms. Ellie is great. We'll just play up his being in class with Owen. Besides, the first day is only an hour and a half. He'll be fine."

I smiled, appreciating her use of the word "we." Adalyn was right. After tossing and turning all night and worrying all morning, I watched Jack hang his red and brown monkey backpack in his cubby and dash into the "Gold Room" with an eerily mature backward wave. I turned to Adalyn with a wide smile.

"All that worrying for nothing!" I laughed.

"See, what did I tell you. Want to go upstairs to the café and get coffee to celebrate?"

"Yes!"

Making sure I was out of sight, I peeked through the narrow window of the classroom before following Adalyn down the hall through the double doors that led to the staircase. Jack was rolling the garbage truck across the rug adorned with the alphabet in primary colors, chattering to Owen the whole time.

"I'm so glad they're in class together. I can't believe they've been friends since they were one," I told Adalyn as the double doors locked behind us, suddenly filled with first-day-of-preschool nostalgia.

"I know."

I tapped my salted caramel mocha to Adalyn's pumpkin Frappuccino. "To a successful first day of preschool."

"Cheers."

Adalyn and I spent the next hour and a half savoring our coffees, obsessing over how weird it was to be without kids for a full ninety minutes, and reminiscing. I wondered how Jack was doing. I checked my phone every few minutes, expecting a call that he was inconsolable, and I'd have to come get him. It never came. He was all smiles when I picked him up, somehow flinging himself into my arms and thrusting something covered in glitter at me simultaneously.

"How was your first day, Jack?"

"Good! Can Owen and I play on the hill outside?"

"Bye, Jack. Bye, Owen." A little boy with a thick head of auburn hair waved on the way out.

I exhaled, but not fully. He'd had successes at the park district, but all summer they'd been interspersed with unsuccessful attempts at attending. Would the same thing happen in preschool?

As it turned out, Jack completed two years of preschool with hardly the off day. I received good behavior reports from Jack's teachers. They had no concerns. I was anxious for our first parent-teacher conference.

"Jack is a joy to have in class," Ms. Ellie told Luke and me. She tucked a strand of honey blond hair behind her ear.

"Any behavior issues?" I wondered how the woman managed to keep her jeans so white.

She smiled. "None whatsoever."

Luke and I looked at each other. I shifted in the miniature blue chair.

Ms. Ellie looked from one of us to the other. "I take it that's not the case at home?"

Luke smiled. "Well, not always."

"He was a really easygoing baby and toddler. Since he turned three, well, he'll go weeks being his easy, compliant self, and then he'll have spurts of defiance and destructiveness."

She smiled again. "Oh, that's normal. It's a big year for them."

"Normal." "Typical." "Adjustment." "Phase." These were words we heard frequently. Each time they were tossed my way I tried to grasp them, to hold them to me like a security blanket, but like sand they sifted through my outstretched fingers.

Still, Jack did more than adjust to preschool. He thrived. Even on days when Owen was absent, he went in without a fuss, giving a smiling hello to his teachers. In fact, it was often difficult to pry him out of the building. His adjustment to school was an enormous relief, and for a while we unclenched our fists.

Until kindergarten when life threw us another curveball.

10

⌘

JACK'S EYES

The eye is the lamp of the body; so then if your eye
is clear, your whole body will be full of light.
—Matthew 6:22

February 16, 2013

Although unable to recall the exact moment of Jack's abduction, the moment I knew will be forever etched in my memory—a jagged scar across my frontal lobe. That night I sat sentry in my three-and-a-half-year-old's room. Plastered against his bedroom door barricaded in with him like some kind of bizarre hostage situation, I watched, shocked, while he tested the hardness of each book against his hand, calculating its potential for inflicting harm before hurling it at my face.

I remember his eyes as he tapped a hard cover on his palm, muttering to himself. His eyes, so bright and blue, were almost taken over by inky pupils. They were unfocused, unfeeling, cold. I don't have adequate words to describe the change. I was terrified of my three-year-old, thirty-pound child. This child wasn't Jack.

The storm had started an hour before, maybe two. Time was part of the physical, orderly world I'd previously known. Luke was out of town on business. It was dead winter, and Jack was restless. My mom was over, and she suggested we get out of the house. It was almost dinner time, so we decided to go to a nearby restaurant with loud games and greasy pizza.

Jack loved this idea. He jumped up and down reminding us that the pizza at Huck's was far superior. That's how Jack talked at three. His preschool teacher told me they were unable to chart the developmental level of his vocabulary because he spoke on the same plane as an adult. His peers didn't always understand him.

Anyway, Jack bounced up and down chattering about the games he'd play and the tickets he'd win, reminding us that it was okay to eat pizza once in a while as long as it's not every day and you still eat your fruit. My mom folded the last few items from the dryer while I buckled my two-month-old into his car seat, breathing a sigh of relief when he didn't immediately start wailing.

Unlike Jack, TJ was a high-needs baby. Where Jack slept five-six hours a night just home from the hospital, TJ never slept more than ninety minutes at a stretch. He needed constant motion and touch, never content to sleep in his crib. I'd walk the floors with him, watching the florescent minutes pass on the oven clock, making a repetitive circle around our first floor. Luke travelled semifrequently then, but this was his first week-long trip since TJ's birth. I'd been dreading it more than usual given the zombielike quality of those newborn days on steroids coupled with Jack's recently manifested behavior problems.

I surveyed the evening. My mom was doing my laundry, we'd found something to kill the time and please Jack, and TJ was sleeping peacefully in his car seat, which was itself a miracle. It seemed today at least would end smoothly.

I left TJ's car seat on the kitchen floor while I squeezed by my mom in the narrow laundry room to get my boots, calling to Jack to do the same. His mop of brown hair appeared in the doorway. He was smiling, but it was different from the excited smile he'd worn a second previously. Well, no, the smile wasn't different. His eyes were. Something about his expression sent a chill through me.

"What?" I said.

Without warning, Jack bolted into the laundry room and charged at my mom, who was straightening the pile of laundry on top of the dryer. His little fists clenched, he punched her in the stomach.

My mom gasped, the shirt she was holding falling to the linoleum. "Jack! That's not like you! Why would you do that to Grandma Margaret!"

Jack was already gearing up for another blow, his fists held in front of him like a pint-sized boxer. Shocked, I grabbed Jack's wrists. He writhed in my grasp, growls of rage shaking his body. My mom was right; this wasn't like Jack. Jack was gentle. He rescued worms drying out on the sidewalk. I was not allowed to squash the yellow tree spiders always sneaking into our home because "they're God's creatures." He was the kid who fished plastic water bottles out of the garbage and lectured us about how long it took one plastic bottle to break down in a landfill (six million years, apparently). I wouldn't believe Jack was capable of an unprovoked attack on his beloved Grandma had I not seen it with my own eyes.

"Jack, we don't hit! You know better. Now we'll have to sit in a time-out."

Jack shrieked so loud I feared the neighbors would hear. "No! You said we were going to Huck's! You're a liar!"

"We can't go to Huck's until you apologize to Grandma," I said with as much restraint as possible. I guided Jack out of the laundry room, back through the kitchen, to the blue plastic Mickey Mouse chair against the half wall separating the dining room and kitchen.

"Three minutes," I announced, still operating under the notion that run of the mill discipline was an efficient response. Turns out I was coming at a forest fire with a squirt gun. I wrestled Jack's rigid body into the chair and turned to set the timer on the oven. That's when all hell broke loose.

Jack shot out of the chair so fast the plastic clattered to the wood floor. He picked it up over his head and hurled it as hard as he could at the wall.

"Okay, I'm restarting the—" I began, still naively convinced I could salvage the night with some firm parenting and a teachable moment. There was no teaching. There was no reasoning. Jack was beyond that. It wasn't the first storm we'd weathered. There'd been many since Jack's third birthday eight months prior. None, though, had been this severe.

Jack charged, wild-eyed, through the kitchen, zeroing in on his baby brother still blissfully dreaming in his car seat. A single step led from our kitchen down into our family room. Jack grabbed the bottom of the car seat and pulled up. Instinct took over, and I lunged, catching the car seat as it tipped backward over the edge of the step, propelled by Jack's force.

My heart pounded in my chest as I righted TJ, who was thankfully strapped in and mercifully still asleep. An only child for three and a half years, Jack had been struggling to adjust to the baby. We'd been telling ourselves a story—the meltdowns, defiance, and aggression that had seemingly cropped up out of nowhere during the first trimester of my pregnancy, shortly after his third birthday were a reaction to this major change in Jack's life. But how often does life gift you with predictable story lines and happy endings?

Others told us it was a phase; the "terrible threes."

"Everyone warned me about the terrible twos," my mom would lament, "but your brother was perfect until he turned three."

"He's perfect in school." His teacher smiled. "They always save the worst for Mom."

Jack was our first child. We hadn't been through the preschool years before. Yes, it was a phase, I assured myself. He'd grow out of it. He was testing the limits. We just had to be firm and consistent, and make sure he was getting adequate one on one attention. I was worrying too much. I always do this...

These were the lines I fed myself in the months leading up to the night of the aborted Huck's trip. I'd almost managed to convince myself, clinging with bloody fingers to the notion that this was all "normal," and my sweet boy would shake off this phase and return to himself.

Luke behaved similarly. "There's nothing wrong with my son," he'd declare. I wanted to believe him. But I couldn't evict the nagging voice in my head.

They say there are no atheists in a foxhole. I launched into survival mode as Jack tore in a circle around the house, grabbing and throwing, tearing, or breaking anything he could get his hands on in his frenzy, his wide eyes zeroing in on each object.

I think the only way you survive in these situations is to switch to autopilot. Quickly, I whisked TJ upstairs and transferred him to his crib, saying a little prayer that he wouldn't wake as he usually did. Panic nearly paralyzed me. How was I going to care for a newborn and keep Jack from destroying the house or hurting someone?

"Hope!" my mom called from downstairs. I turned toward the note of warning in her voice. TJ's room is right at the top of the stairs. When I turned, I came face to face with Jack flying up them, his feet not appearing to touch the steps. His eyes were trained on the crib. I positioned myself between them and herded Jack out of the room with my body while he raged and scratched at me. He lunged at the door while I yanked it shut.

Jack pivoted at the top of the stairs, charging back down to continue his tornadolike rampage of the first floor. With TJ safely enclosed in his room, I pursued Jack, desperate to snap him out of whatever fog was possessing him. If I could just talk to him, find out what was bothering him...

I caught up to him in the living room, tearing up paper. He simultaneously shrieked and laughed when he saw me, sweeping the hand-painted wooden candle holders we'd gotten from Thailand and the cheap Ikea lamp off the end table like a miniature Hulk. I foiled his attempt to dart past me, lifting him to the air and collapsing on the couch.

This was it. I'd look into his eyes. We'd communicate. Obviously, time-out hadn't worked. I just had to get to the root of this, whatever *this* was. It was far beyond the definition of a tantrum. Acting out was too tame a phrase. Even misbehavior couldn't describe what was happening. Now I know what we were dealing with that cold winter night is called a flare, and every method I employed was futile. I was blowing into the wind.

I had a dusty degree in psychology, I figured; I should know how to diffuse the situation. I sat Jack on my lap facing me and stared intently into his eyes, searching the murky pupils for my son.

"Jack." My tone was pleading rather than assertive as I'd planned. "What's going on? This isn't you. You're my sweet boy. Let's calm—"

The eerie smile never left Jack's face. He gave no indication that my words were permeating his consciousness. My son reared back and spit in my face. Disbelief. Shock. Frustration. Anger. The disrespect. How dare he?

Like most in my generation, I was raised to have respect and healthy fear. Never in my wildest, most rebellious imagination would I have even visualized spitting at *anyone*, much less an adult, much less my parent. Where had I gone wrong?

I'm ashamed to admit what I tried next. I set Jack down, walked to the fridge, touched the tip of my pinky to the tip of a bottle of taco sauce, and touched it to Jack's offending mouth. My three-year-old. Why? I thought it was time for tough love. I thought Jack was careening down some path of delinquent behavior, and I had to put my foot down. I wish I'd known. I wish I'd put discipline aside to wait out the storm. I wish I could've identified the storm. At the time, though, I didn't know what I didn't know. It's a moment for which I have to choose grace and forgiveness for myself every single day.

I was in uncharted territory, and I was afraid. I had a baby to protect and a bewildered Grandma as a witness. I was afraid for Jack, and I was afraid of Jack. I feared for my own safety. I was afraid of my three-year-old child.

"Hope!" my mom gasped. "That's so unlike you, to do something like that! Get him a popsicle!"

None of this was like anything. Jack, who'd reacted to my uncharacteristic discipline with more spitting, switched to crying for a popsicle.

"No," I said robotically, unsure if I was more shocked by Jack's behavior or my own. "I'll get you some milk."

I sat on the couch and rocked Jack while he drank his sippy cup of milk. Maybe this was it. Maybe the regrettable discipline I'd employed had at least shocked him out of his fugue. "I'm sorry I put the hot sauce on your mouth," I said softly. "I want to know what's going on. I was so surprised when you spit at me."

Jack turned in my lap to face me. He smiled, milk dribbling down his chin. Then he took another drink, held the milk in his mouth, and spit it. I raised my arm to shield my eyes from the spray, realizing I was still wearing my coat. Jack took advantage of my distraction and propelled himself off my lap heading upstairs.

"Jack, talk to us, hunny." My mom made an unsuccessful attempt to intercept Jack.

I shed my coat, wiped my eyes, and followed Jack up the stairs. He marched past TJ's room and headed down the hall to his own room. I stuck my hand in the door as he was slamming it shut.

"Ahhh!" Jack stormed over to his bookshelf against the wall and began to extract books.

I pulled the door shut and sat on the floor with my back up against it, trying to contain this. Trying to contain Jack. Muttering to himself, Jack pulled a hard cover copy of *The Very Hungry Caterpillar* off the wooden shelf opened his left palm, and struck the book against it, nodding to himself. Jack loved that book. It was a pop-up book, the fruit tattered from so many repetitions. The beloved book became a weapon. Jack looked up at me, his eyes far away. He lunged at me, flinging the book at my face. I put my hand up just in time to dodge the blow.

Shock does not encompass what I felt. Even heartbreak is too tame a term. I couldn't reconcile this vacant-eyed child with my sweet, sensitive Jack. He was gone. I fought the tears stinging my eyes as Jack tested each beloved story book before flinging it at me. *Richard Scary. Dr. Seuss. Go, Dog, Go.* These were books I read to Jack while we sat side by side in the loft on the miniature upholstered couch I'd retreat to as a child. The couch and its matching rocker sat in a corner of our loft next to a small square bookshelf and bin overflowing with books. We called it "book nook." We sat in book nook before bed, me balancing books on my growing belly, and then juggling them around a nursing baby. I'd tried. I'd tried to keep our routines the same, to keep playing with and reading to Jack just as much so he wouldn't feel jealous. Yet as I sat on the carpeted floor numbly blocking books from hitting my face, I knew this was more than jealousy. It was more than adjusting to a new brother. It was far beyond the terrible threes.

I didn't try to touch Jack or talk to him. I didn't try to stop him. I couldn't. The safest thing was to keep him contained—barricade myself in this room with him. I was afraid.

Eventually, Jack exhausted himself. Eventually, he lay down on the carpet amidst strewn books—the carnage of a natural disaster. We stayed like that; no one speaking, no one moving. I couldn't go to him. I feared any movement would set him off again. I was paralyzed.

Then TJ's hunger cry reached me from the room down the hall. Fortunately, he'd slept through Jack's rampage. I looked at Jack. My run-of-the-mill nervous anticipation juggling the needs of an infant and preschooler had not included this scenario. Jack didn't move. TJ's cries became more insistent.

I got up slowly, stiffly, surveying the room. Then I crept down the hall and opened TJ's door. His face was red, his miniature fists clenched in angry balls. I gently lifted him from the crib, kissing the dark soft fuzz on his nearly bald head. "Mommy's here," I crooned. I changed TJ's diaper and settled into the rocking chair to nurse. His distress I could easily define. This at least I could fix.

Mothers are supposed to, aren't they? They're supposed to anticipate their children's needs and fix them. I watched TJ's eyes close, his little fist nestled on my chest. I listened to the music of his satisfied swallows, listening also for Jack.

My mom came in holding my cell phone out. "It's Luke." She handed me the phone and looked over her shoulder. "Where's Jack?"

"In his room," I answered before turning my attention to the phone.

"Hi, how's your evening going?" Luke's voice asked.

His voice unleashed the tears I'd been holding. "Something is wrong with Jack," I whispered into the phone. "He tried to knock TJ's carrier over with him in it. He punched my mom. He threw books at me and spit at me. I—I feel so bad, I put hot sauce on his tongue. What kind of a mother does that?"

"Hun, hun, it's okay. I'm sure you were at your wits end. I'll be home tomorrow."

"But I don't know what to do tonight."

"Want me to talk to him?"

"He's in his room. I think he's calming down. I'm in here with TJ."

"Well, good. I know, it's tough, hun, but he'll adjust."

I felt a familiar frustration building within me. Luke wasn't here, and I couldn't adequately explain what I was dealing with. I was about to continue my whispered revelations that something was really going on, but I heard a creak. I listened silently as Jack's footsteps padded down the hallway. He entered the room. I couldn't help it. I flinched.

"Jack, Mommy's upset," my mom said. I'd forgotten she was still standing in the doorway.

Jack looked at my tearstained face, came over, laid his head on my arm, and patted first me then his baby brother. I looked in his eyes. They were red-rimmed, tired, and sorrowful, but the coldness was gone. The storm had passed as suddenly as it had arrived.

Everything had changed, though. The thick, warm, comforting blanket of denial had been ripped clear of my shoulders. That night I knew. I knew it in a way I could never unknow it.

Something is wrong with my child.

11

❧ ❧ ❧

THE BIG DAY

So teach us to number our days so we may gain a heart of wisdom.
—Psalm 90:12

August–September 2014

Jack's teacher read Dr. Seuss's *Oh, The Places You'll Go!* to the class on the last day of school. After the story was over, she wiped her eyes and called each child up for a hug and a plastic gold metal placed around their neck. Cameras flashed. He may as well have been graduating college for all the pride, joy, and relief I felt.

It was tough to say goodbye to Good Shepherd Preschool. It wasn't really goodbye, I reasoned. Jack's little brother would attend. The summer before Jack began kindergarten was filled with play-dates, pool days, and parks. The boys kept me busy. Jack was five and TJ was two and a half. TJ had advanced from crawling to running at fifteen months old, and once he started running, he never seemed to stop. I'd get halfway through my first sentence to a friend at the park before dashing after TJ, who was making a beeline for the sidewalk, attempting to ditch the park scene.

Jack functioned typically for such long stretches it seemed the worst was behind us. But every good day, though cherished, was a temporary reprieve. I'll never forget the look on Luke's face when he saw Jack have an episode mirroring the one Jack had the night he threw the books at my face. I recognized it. Shock, disbelief, confusion, anger, and heartbreak.

The summer leading up to kindergarten was shrouded in déjà vu. As weeks went by, anticipation of Jack's first day of kindergarten grew. His success in preschool gave us confidence, and he seemed excited to start "big boy" school.

When the big day came, we rushed through our usual morning routine. I forgot to run a brush through my hair before rushing out the door juggling a two-year-old, a five-year-old, a backpack, and a diaper bag. I buckled the boys into their car seats and headed for Saint Agnus Catholic School. Both boys had been baptized at the church there. Adalyn and I had run the mom's group for a year. We attended mass every week and knew the priests. It felt surreal, finally dropping Jack off for school.

On the first day, parents were allowed to walk students in. Jack smiled on the front steps under the big black letters spelling out *Saint Agnus Catholic School* on the stone wall. I chased TJ down the hall and accidentally whacked at least one child with my black diaper bag. Jack pointed proudly at the laminated school bus nameplate designating his locker. A locker! I couldn't believe my little boy had a locker. I'd imagined this day since he'd been baptized in the adjoining church. I took a picture of him next to his locker, a picture of Jack and TJ, and a picture of Jack with his teacher, Mrs. TwentyfiveYearsExperience. *Click, click, click.* I posted the pictures on social media with the caption, *first day of kindergarten* along with many other parents. When it was time for TJ and me to leave I scooped him up and tried to ignore the tension in my spine.

"See you in a few hours, Jack. Remember, it's only half days this week."

"Okay, bye!" Jack waved.

"He'll do fine," Mrs. TwentyfiveYearsExperience said, practically shutting the door in my face.

I had no time to peek through the window this time, as TJ was bolting back down the hallway.

"TJ, wait for Mommy!" He didn't even slow down. I caught up to him, and we ran hand in hand to the car.

I fiddled with the radio while I tried to capture my thoughts. I dialed Luke's number.

"How'd it go?" Luke answered.

"Great. He didn't cry. No problems with me leaving. I'll send you the pictures."

"Great, hun. I was hopeful he'd be excited about it. He did so well in preschool."

"I'm relieved. We still can't leave him with a sitter, even grandparents, and park district classes didn't go so well this summer. I'm really glad he had a good first day. I wish you could've seen him."

"Me too hun. Send me those pictures. What are you and TJ going to do?"

TJ kicked the back of my seat excitedly as I pulled up to the park. It was rare for us to get one on one time. "We're going to play at the park and walk around the neighborhood. I pick Jack up at eleven thirty, and I'll let him choose where to go for lunch."

"Have a good day."

I ended the call and rummaged in my bag through graham cracker crumbs and monster trucks for my drug store sunglasses. TJ was already in Houdini mode, wiggling his arms free of his five-point harness.

"Wait for Mom, TJ."

TJ alternated between playing in the sand and running down the sidewalk. I pushed him in the swing, gave him a snack, and settled him in the green and gray double stroller for a long walk through the neighbor. It was a beautiful, sunny day on a perfect tree-lined street. I tried to stay present with TJ and not spend every moment wondering what Jack was doing. TJ was restless. Finally, I relented and let him stand in front of me and "help" me push the stroller.

I pulled back into the parking lot at eleven fifteen, experiencing momentary panic when I saw the lines of cars. Apparently, there was a very efficient system. The kids were dismissed by grade and the cars pulled up to a row of cones by the door. Jack climbed into the Santa Fe with his hands full of drawings.

"How was school, Jack?" I asked, my voice too loud.

"Jack!" TJ said.

"It was good," Jack said. "Kinda long."

I hoped he'd adjust in the next four days. The following week they transitioned to full six-hour school days.

"But we were learning *colors*," Jack continued, his voice indignant. "And how to write our names. I already know that."

I smiled. "It's the first day, Jack. All kids know different things going into kindergarten. They'll start with review, but you'll learn so much."

The rest of the week progressed without incident. Jack's sole complaint was that kindergarten was too easy. I signed up for lunchroom duties and the first field trip. TJ and I fell into a comfortable routine. Everything was fine. Great, even.

But it didn't last.

12

STOLEN MILESTONE

"But whoever causes one of these little ones who believe in Me
to stumble, it would be better for him to have a heavy millstone
hung around his neck, and to be drown in the depths of the sea."
—Matthew 18:6

September 2014

I pulled the Santa Fe into the now-familiar pick-up line and rubbed
my temples. TJ had screamed through most of the trip, making the
fifteen-minute drive seem three times that long. He'd finally dozed
off in his car seat. I turned the music down and sighed, indulging in
the small window of quiet before the school doors opened.

Jack had a full week of kindergarten under his belt. It was his
first full day of school, and I was anxious how he'd enjoyed it. Other
than some extra tiredness, Jack had taken to kindergarten, though he
maintained he "already knew what they were teaching."

I looked at the clock on the dash. I couldn't believe Jack had
been away from me for a full six and half hours. My big boy. I glanced
in the rearview mirror at TJ. His little head was tipped to the side, his
impossibly long eyelashes brushed his cheek. A trail of drool dripped
from his chin onto the collar of his yellow shirt. A wave of nostalgia
washed through me.

I craned my neck as the kindergartners filed onto the sidewalk on the side of the school. Jack was one of the last ones out. His backpack was slung carelessly over his shoulder, partially unzipped. He wore a tired frown on his little face. I got out of the car, smiled, and waved. Jack gave me a half wave and trudged to the car.

"How was your first full day? You're such a big boy now!" I whisper-yelled as we got settled into the car.

Jack's face in the rearview mirror was obscured while he bent his head to rummage in his backpack. I tapped my fingers on the steering wheel as I waited for the line of cars to move. Jack wrestled his stink bug lunch box out of his backpack. I heard a zip and a clink as he extracted his blue thermos and spoon.

"Jack, hunny, don't eat that mac and cheese now. It's been sitting all day. It's not good anymore." Never mind what unleashed mac and cheese would do to the back of my car. "Didn't you eat your lunch?"

"No. We didn't have enough time. We had, like, a minute, and then the lunch ladies were like, 'kindergarten, it's time to go out for recess.' I had no time!"

"I'm sure you had more than a minute, Jack."

"No, I didn't!"

"Shh!" I glanced in the rearview mirror at TJ, who stirred but didn't wake.

"You asked." Jack crossed his little arms over his chest, the open thermos tilting precariously in his lap.

"Okay. You can have something when we get home."

"I'll just eat my animal crackers." More rummaging, and then crunching came from the back seat.

"You didn't have time for morning snack?"

"My tummy was hurting. Now it's hurting because it's hungry."

"I'm sorry. I can make you a PBJ when we get home. Were you nervous today?"

"No!"

"Okay, just asking. Did you have an okay day otherwise?"

Jack was quiet for a moment. "It was long."

I nodded. "It's your longest day of school so far. But you're doing great. You'll get used to it, and it won't seem as long."

"I liked last week better," he said softly.

I was about to respond when I heard TJ gurgle. "Nack!" he said.

"Stop! I don't feel like talking right now."

I frowned. "Jack, your brother missed you. I missed you too."

Jack perked up after we arrived home, and he devoured a sandwich. He was still out of sorts, but we played in the backyard, and he settled down for a show while I cleaned out his lunch box and went through his red folder. I pulled out a picture of a bird and smiled at the childish red coloring. Then I looked at the top of the page.

"Try to stay in the lines," Mrs. TwentyfiveYearsExperience had written in red pen. I studied the picture. It wasn't scribbled carelessly. In fact, in only a few spots the red crayon crept over the black outline. The bird was completely filled in. I thought of the sweet, encouraging notes Jack's preschool teachers had written on each precious drawing. I glanced at my five-year-old on the couch with a cup of cheddar bunnies and his snuggle blankie. I looked back down at the picture in my hand. The picture I was going to hang on the fridge. I understood challenging kids to do their best, but Jack's coloring wasn't careless.

A live wire of anger zapped through me at Mrs. TwentyfiveYearsExperience. Jack was a young five, his birthday being in June. Many of the boys in his class had already turned six. We considered holding him back a year, but we worried he'd be bored. He wanted to go to kindergarten, and he'd been so successful in preschool. Plus, academically he was ahead. This was a coloring sheet—on day six of kindergarten. I'm not a parent to go raise hell at the school to get my kid a different grade or anything, but I wondered, was it necessary to write a comment on staying in the lines, especially at the very beginning of the school year? Jack was a proficient reader. Did Mrs. TwentyfiveYearsExperience's comment have anything to do with Jack' sour mood, or was he simply tired from the full day? *It's a kindergarten coloring sheet*, I thought, *not the SATs*.

"Mommy, do I have school tomorrow?" Jack yawned as I tucked him into bed that night.

"Yes, Bean, tomorrow's Tuesday."

"Oh no! It's only the second day of the week! I don't wanna go!"

I pushed aside the pang I felt. I wanted Jack to be happy at his new school. My expectations were probably too high for only the second week of school. Full days were bound to be an adjustment.

"I know, Bean, but you get hot lunch tomorrow. You've been excited to get hot lunch."

He nodded, his eyelids fluttering.

Once the kids were asleep, I showed Luke Jack's coloring sheet with the teacher's comment.

Luke shook his head. "Wow, kindergarten sure has changed since we were kids."

"Isn't that ridiculous? He's five."

Luke popped open a beer. "Well, people who can't color inside the lines don't get into Harvard." He grinned at me.

"I just hope she's the right teacher for him. Betsy Smith—her daughter's in second grade—told me she's great, much more experienced than the other kindergarten teacher. She's just so different from the teachers at Good Shepherd."

"He'll adjust. He's only been in kindergarten for six days."

I nodded. "I know. I'm sure you're right. I just don't want her to break his spirit."

"No, nothing will break his fiery spirit. I did the chores. Come sit with me and let's watch something."

We were still in the process of selecting a show when TJ's cries emanated from the baby monitor. "Mama-mama!"

I sighed. "Impeccable timing as always." I rose and stretched.

"Sorry, hun. Want me to get him?"

"It's okay." I knew TJ would want me. Though he'd stopped nursing, TJ still woke frequently and screamed until I cradled and rocked him. TJ was a snuggler. He liked to run his little hand across my arm while we rocked. He needed constant motion. Still at two I often resorted to walking the floors with him throughout the night, as I had since his birth. My mom and many others tried to persuade me to let him "cry it out." At two and a half, he was well beyond needing milk during the night. Still, it never felt quite right with TJ. I was up with him several times that night.

I dragged myself out of bed on Tuesday morning. The boys were equally difficult to pry from their slumber.

"I don't wanna go to school today. I'm sick," Jack whined, laying across the kitchen chair while his waffles cooled.

I touched his forehead with one hand and shoved his folder into his backpack with the other. "You feel cool. Eat your waffles."

"I'm not hungry."

"You can take them in the car." Luke pushed Jack's dark hair back and kissed his forehead. "Bye, bud." He moved on to TJ who was eating banana slices and cheerios off his highchair tray. "Bye, TJ. Have a good day with Mom. Love you, guys."

He gave me a quick kiss and hurried out. I watched from the front window as he rode away on his bike, an uneasy feeling in my stomach.

"All right, come on guys, we have to go." I mopped TJ's face and made a mental note to clean up the banana mashed into the seat of his highchair.

I managed to wipe most of the banana from TJ's face and hair, briefly wondering if any had actually made it into his mouth. I slid TJ's sandals on while fantasizing about stopping at Starbucks after dropping Jack off. After yet another night of disrupted sleep, I could almost taste my venti mocha with a much-needed extra shot.

"Jack, come on! Get your shoes on. We have to go. Where are you?" Jack had disappeared. An edge of panic crept into my tired veins. We were going to be late if we didn't hurry. "Jack? Jack!"

"Wait right here," I said to TJ, imagining for a moment that it was realistic to expect a two-year-old to remain sedentary. Jack was not in the bathroom, the living room, or the family room. After I raced through the first floor, I dashed upstairs in a frenzy of stress and irritation. "Jack, this is not funny! We have to go!"

I searched his room, TJ's room and the playroom. Finally, I found him hiding under the queen bed in our bedroom. "Jack, what are you doing, Bean? What's wrong? It's time to leave for school."

TJ, who had followed me on my quest, grabbed Jack's feet sticking out from under the bed. Jack squealed, sending TJ into a fit of giggles.

"Come on," I sighed. "You're going to get your uniform all wrinkled."

"I don't care. I don't want to go to school!" Jack's muffled voice came from under the bed.

"Jack, come out here so we can talk. Did something happen at school to upset you?"

"No. It's boring and long, and I don't want to go."

"Hunny, I know it's long. It's only your second week. It'll get easier." I paused. "Are you sure nothing happened? You can tell me."

"No, nothing happened. I just don't wanna go."

Somehow, I coaxed Jack out from under the bed. His body went limp when I took his hand to lead him downstairs. My back protested when I lifted his dead weight into my arms. I got Jack into his car seat. By the time I buckled TJ in on the other side, Jack had unbuckled his own five-point harness. I dashed back around to the other side.

"Jack, we need to be safe." Beads of sweat rolled down my back. I struggled to rebuckle the harness while Jack tried just as hard to thwart my efforts. We were both tired, cranky, and near tears by the time we pulled out of the garage.

"I'm mad at you," was all Jack would say when I tried to prod him for more information.

"Mad!" TJ announced in apparent solidarity.

I rubbed the back of my neck where a knot of tension was forming. The drop-off-line had cleared by the time I pulled my Santa Fe into the deserted lot. Typically, cars pulled around to the side door of the school in a line. Parents remained in their cars while a teacher or aid led each child from car to building. If you missed the first bell, parents had to park and walk their children into the office. I wrangled the boys out of the car, hoisted TJ onto my hip, and took ahold of Jack's hand. Jack dragged his feet. I felt my face grow hot as we made the walk of shame into the attendance office.

The young woman at the front desk offered a saccharine smile when she buzzed us in. Her long black hair hung in silky strands down her shoulders. She wore a crisp white blouse. "Who do we have here?" She raised her eyebrows at Jack then sized me up.

In that moment, I saw myself through her eyes: messy hair, jeans torn at the knee, toddler on my hip. Late on the seventh day of school. "Jack Shepherd."

She poked a lime green acrylic nail at her screen. "Oh, you're in Mrs. TwentyfiveYearsExperience's class. Since you're in kindergarten, we'll give you a pass, but let's try to be on time, kay?" She looked at me. "It disrupts the class when students walk in late."

I said nothing, taking the blue Post-It she thrust at me. I walked Jack down the long hallway, TJ squirming in my arms. Jack struggled with his locker door and then silently hung his backpack on the hook. He stopped, staring at the half window in his classroom door.

"Go ahead and knock, Jack," I said, knowing the classroom doors were locked for security.

Jack shook his head. I opened my mouth to repeat my request when Mrs. TwentyfiveYearsExperience caught sight of us. She plastered on a smile eerily similar to that worn by Front Desk Lady and opened the door. "Good morning, Jack."

Jack turned and reached toward me. I squeezed his hand. "Have a good day, Jack. Love you."

"No! I want to go home!" Jack gripped my fingers.

The teacher frowned at me. "It's better if you can avoid walking him in."

"I'm sorry. We had a little trouble getting out of the house this morning," I answered, offering the understatement of the year.

"He'll be fine." She seized Jack's wrist and guided him into the classroom. "Come on, Jack. Class is starting. Bye, Mom." She closed the door behind them.

I could hear Jack's cries through the plexiglass. *He'll be fine.* I blew a kiss and forced myself not to linger, which would only make things worse.

*****

"How was hot lunch today?" I asked Jack when he got into the backseat that afternoon, choosing to focus on something positive, hoping my attitude would transfer to Jack.

Jack wrinkled his nose. "Bad."

"Wasn't it pancakes today? They didn't taste good?" I'd assumed pancakes for lunch would serve as a special treat.

"I don't know. I didn't taste them."

"Then how do you know they weren't good?" I tried to keep the exasperation out of my voice.

"It smelled in the lunchroom."

"Like what? Syrup?" I tried to conjure up memories of school lunchroom smells, but I must have blocked them out.

"I don't know," Jack whined. It just smelled like a lot."

I stopped myself from reminding Jack we had paid for the hot lunch. "Well, what else happened today?"

"I went to the nurse's office."

"What?" I put my left blinker on. "They didn't call me."

Jack kicked the seat in front of him. "She said I had to go back to class once lunch was over."

"You went during lunch?"

"Yeah. It smelled like a lot in the lunchroom. And I didn't want to go outside for recess."

"Why not?"

"My tummy hurt, and bees are out."

I sighed. "I'm sorry, Jack. Tomorrow will be better."

The next day was not better. The transition out of the house was smoother, and we managed to arrive on time, but once a nice mom volunteer came to the car to walk Jack to class, he threw his body over the center seat and grabbed TJ's car seat. "No! I want you to walk me in! I want you to walk me in, Mom!"

"Jack, you know the rules. Parents can't walk the kids in after the first week. Mrs. Smith will walk you right to class."

"Yep!" the poor, bewildered mom said brightly. She unbuckled his harness. Jack clung to TJ's car seat for dear life, continuing to scream that he wanted me to walk him in. TJ began his own screaming, trying to pry Jack's fingers off his car seat. Mrs. Smith's smile disappeared. She looked worriedly behind her at the backed-up line. "I think you're going to need to park and walk him in, Mom."

I wasn't supposed to, but what choice did I have? The poor lady had tried to coax him. I parked and turned back to Jack. "Okay, I'll walk you in today, but tomorrow you have to get out of the car in the drop off lane." I felt like I was giving in.

Jack nodded solemnly and took my hand. So much of parenting is repeating the same action over and over again, day after day. I hoisted TJ onto my hip, clicked the lock button on my key ring, and took Jack's hand, hustling him into the building. I hurried him along, having no desire for another encounter with Front Desk Lady and a tardy slip. Fortunately, we had just enough time to make it to Jack's classroom before the bell rang.

"Come on, Jack, the bell's about to ring!" Mrs. TwentyfiveYearsExperience called as students hurried in around her.

Jack fumbled to get his backpack into his locker. TJ yanked a lock of my hair. Jack turned at me, his eyes brimming with tears. My heart wrenched. Every part of me wanted to grab him, run out of the building, and bring him home to snuggle up on the couch with books. Maybe I should have. But the teacher was already guiding him into the room.

"It's best not to walk him in, Mom. It just makes the separation harder. He'll be fine."

I opened my mouth to explain, but her back was already turned.

"Why is he crying?" a little girl's voice floated through the closing door.

I carried TJ back to the car and did some crying of my own on the drive home. My heart wrenched with guilt. I felt Jack's sadness and anxiety at my core. I read somewhere once that you can only be as happy as your unhappiest child. That morning I felt Jack's unhappiness acutely. I thought of him all day, looking at the clock and wondering what he was doing. I thought of him while TJ and I played outside in the shade of the oak tree. When I put TJ down for his nap, I looked at the clock and my stomach hurt. It was lunch time at Saint Agnus. Would Jack go to the nurse's office? Would they call me if he did? Pulling the curtains closed against the brilliant early-afternoon sun I crawled into my own bed. Pictures of Jack scared and upset, making himself as small as possible on the cold metal bench in the lunchroom, haunted me. My tears trickled onto the pillow. *He'll adjust. He'll be fine.*

The rest of the week unfolded in carbon copies of that day. My car would remain in the lot after all the other parents had dropped off their kids and moved on. Each morning, I endured snide commentary from Front Desk Lady and reminders that it was really better if Jack walked in himself from Mrs. TwentyfiveYearsExperiene. Each afternoon, Mrs. TwentyfiveYearsExperience trotted up to my waiting car, put her hand on the open window, and said, "He did fine."

Jack's own reports of school were different. It was boring, he said. It was too long. The lunchroom was stinky and loud, and it made his tummy hurt. At home, his meltdowns increased. We put him to bed earlier. I vacillated between wondering if we should've waited an extra year before sending Jack to kindergarten and reminding myself it was only the second week of school.

"I don't want to go back to school." Jack cried that Saturday night.

"It's Saturday. We still have one more day of the weekend."

"Oh no!" Jack's breathing quickened. "I only have one more day until I have to go back to SCHOOL!"

"Hey, it's okay." I rubbed his back. "I know it's hard, Jack. I had a hard time starting kindergarten too. I missed my mom and dad."

Jack wiped his eyes and looked at me, his pupils like saucers. "You did?"

"Yep. But I got used to it and even made some really great friends."

Jack was awake until ten thirty that night, worrying about school.

"Do you think we should've given him an extra year of preschool?" I asked Luke as we got ready for bed.

"I don't think so, hun. He's ahead of his peers academically. He's already saying he's bored. It hasn't been that long. It's just a big change."

I nodded. Jack would have been bored and unhappy watching his classmates go off to kindergarten while he did another year of preschool. Maybe I did need to give him more time to adapt.

The following week I was on lunch duty. Jack's teacher insisted he was fine all day, while Jack reported significant distress, especially during lunch. It left me to wonder, was Jack's initial separation anxiety short-lived? Were his complaints a function of his dichotomous thinking and his little boy tendency to catastrophize? Or was he holding it all together at school, struggling inside all day? I was anxious to catch Jack in the middle of his day. So many times, I pictured his little body at those big long tables, a pensive look on his face.

That Monday, I checked in and got my visitor's pass from Front Desk Lady. "How's your little boy doing?" she asked with a glass smile.

I forced myself to return her smile, commenting that Jack had done well the first week, but had a struggled a bit since then. "Saturday night he was still up at ten thirty worrying about school Monday morning and saying he didn't want to go."

She waved a French-manicured hand. "Oh, please. Teenagers say that." She turned her head and called to the lady with curly red hair sitting in the chair behind her. "Hey, Gwen, do your teenagers ever say they don't want to go to school?" She smiled up at me while waiting for the answer.

Gwen chuckled. "Oh yeah, all the time."

Front Desk Lady's eyes bugged out. "Even on weekends?" I had a feeling she already knew the answer.

"Especially on the weekends." Gwen laughed. "Just wait. Little kids, little problems. Big kids, big problems."

"See, Mom?" Front Desk Lady said. "It's normal. We all have to do things we don't want to do." It was in that moment I pictured dragging her out by her sleek black hair and rubbing her patronizing face into the gravel. Not very Christian of me, I know.

Throughout the day, several responses would go through my head, but in that moment, I simply collected my visitor lanyard and headed to the windowless basement. A steady wall of noise floated up the stairs to greet me; indistinguishable chatter and shrieks of excitement mixed with clattering of hot lunch trays on metal tables. It was a lot. I momentarily regretted not signing up for library duty instead. I could understand Jack getting overstimulated at lunch.

I knew kindergartners were at the table closest to the stairwell. I hung back, just outside the line of vision. There was Jack sitting sandwiched between two little girls immersed in conversation across him. I wanted to catch him eating his lunch, or even better, laughing and chatting with a classmate. Instead, I found Jack sitting stiffly, his shoulders raised, staring down at his untouched lunch. Silent tears dripped down his little face.

My heart wrenching, I approached the table. "Hi, Jack," I said brightly as I reached him. My son looked up at me, his eyes brimming.

"I want to go home," he whispered. "My tummy hurts. I asked to go to the nurse, but Mrs. TwentyfiveYearsExperience said no."

"Are you his mom?" the blond girl beside Jack asked. I nodded. "He's crying."

Thanks, I thought.

"Jack, I'm here for lunch and recess. Why don't you try eating your lunch and see if your tummy feels better?"

Jack stared at the French toast sticks in front of him. "It smells," he said.

Jack's eyes remained trained on me while I hustled around opening juice boxes, cleaning up spills, and tracking down hot lunch orders. I was glad I'd left TJ with my mom this time.

Jack never did touch his food. My sensitive boy who was always so concerned about waste, dumped his tray into the red plastic trash can. When the bell rang for recess, three hundred kindergarten through fifth graders rushed to the stairwell. Jack latched on to me as the stampede entered the stairwell bracketed by volunteers.

"We have to keep up with my class!" Jack pulled me up the stairs through a throng of older kids rushing through a set of doors to the blacktop. "Where are they? They left me behind!"

I caught sight of a blond ponytail. "Right up there." I squeezed Jack's hand. "Jack, you know the playground is just up the stairs and down the hall. You can see where everyone is going."

"Yeah, but they hurry too much. I might get lost."

"You can always ask any of the adults with badges to help." I squinted as we excited the steel doors into the sun. I pointed to a group of boys I recognized from Jack's class. "There, Jack. Why don't you draw chalk with them?"

Jack shrugged and walked over to the other boys. He looked back at me. Soon, Jack was playing with the other boys, and I relaxed a little, standing on the sidelines. Ten minutes later a whistle blew. In an impressively practiced fashion, the students lined up according to class. Jack was at the back of his line. Once the students were counted, they marched back to the doors. Jack looked up at me, a look of unmistakable panic in his blue eyes.

"Can you walk me in?"

"I can walk you to the door," I said brightly. "Then I'll say goodbye. But hey, TJ and I will see you in only two hours."

Jack marched in front of me, stopping dead as we reached the door. Other kids streamed around him. Jack grabbed my hand and shook his head.

"Jack, it's okay. I have to go home now, but I'll be back soon. Just specials left today. You get to go to the library." I gently removed my hand and gave Jack a wave.

Jack lunged for me. "Take me home!" he cried. I heard mutters of annoyance as the rest of the kids funneled past.

"Jack, it's okay. I'll be back before you know it."

"Come on, Jack," the smiling teacher's aide said, sweeping Jack over the threshold. I saw him peeking back at me as the door shut.

He was at school. He was safe. Why did I feel so guilty? My own tears fell on the drive home. My thoughts boomeranged. Maybe being a lunch/recess mom wasn't such a good idea, not that I'd known that when I signed up at orientation. I was signed up for that week and the following. I hoped it wouldn't be this hard on Jack for me to leave again.

That Wednesday I was selected as one of the chaperones on the class fieldtrip to the nearby arboretum. Fortunately, my aunt was available to watch TJ. On the school bus Jack sat a few seats ahead of me with another boy, their heads bobbing up and down. The rubbery smell and rough motion of the bus brought back not so fond memories of my own elementary years. I chatted with the room mother, an energetic blond slightly older than myself. Not far into the conversation, she asked the question I'd come to dread.

"How's Jack liking kindergarten?"

The question always came with a smile and well-meaning; I'd asked it myself when I'd run in to parents from Jack's preschool. I seemed to be the only one with an answer other than "He loves it!"

"Jack did really well the first week. He struggles with the long days. He just turned five in June."

"Does he get tired?" she asked.

I nodded, thinking that tired didn't begin to cover it.

"You know," she continued, "Sara's mother picks her up right before lunch. She says it's a long day for a five-year-old. Sara is her fourth child to attend Saint Agnus. I'm a mother of six myself."

"Sara goes half days? I was told they didn't offer half days here."

"Well, they don't, officially. But they let her pick Sara up before lunch. Maybe, ask the social worker about it for Jack."

"Yeah, I will, thanks." I thought of this option during the rest of the drive and throughout the field trip as I trailed behind Jack and four other boys through blooming hydrangeas. Jack chatted easily with the other boys. I even caught a few giggles. He often checked to make sure I was close by.

I tried to enjoy the beautiful grounds of the arboretum—the warm sun, the fresh flowers, the variety of birds. I retained a constant head count of my charges and participated in snippets of mandatory small talk, but my mind was working overtime. If Jack came home before lunch, would that help him? He'd be missing electives, but it was only kindergarten. It would be worth it if it would help him adjust, especially since lunch seemed to be a big issue. I decided I'd see how the rest of the week went.

"He's having a ball with the other boys," the room mom commented on the bus ride home. Jack was giggling with two other boys.

Jack had done well all day. But when we arrived back at school and corralled the sweaty, grass-smelling kids back into the classroom, Jack tried to barricade the door.

"Jack, I'll be back in an hour. I just have to go home and get TJ so Aunt Dina can go home. School's almost over for today."

Jack shook his head. Mrs. TwentyfiveYearsExperience approached. "Come on, Jack. Mom will be right back."

She guided Jack's rigid body to his table while several classmates looked on.

"See you soon!" I said brightly, making a quick exit to avoid making the situation worse. I caught the sight of Jack fighting tears.

"It's hard, isn't it?" another mom chaperone said to me on the way out. She tucked her short brown hair behind her ears and pulled down her sunglasses.

I smiled. "Yeah. He's had a hard time with separation."

"Is he your first?"

I nodded.

"Chloe's my first. She's a mama's girl. I think it's harder on me than it is on her, though." She laughed. "They'll adjust, right?"

"Yeah." *I hope so.*

I turned my hard rock on loud on the drive home, attempting to drown out thoughts of Jack fighting tears in the classroom as I walked away from him. Why did he seem to be struggling so much more than the other kids? No matter how many times I tried to convince myself Jack just needed to adjust, I was unsettled. Then I did something I hadn't done in years. I stopped at the gas station and bought a pack of cigarettes.

I hadn't smoked since college, but the stress of Jack's struggles and the exhaustion of TJ's still broken nights was taking its toll, and I took advantage of my rare kid-free moments. I hid the Marlboro Lights in my glove compartment, snagging one here or there during TJ's naps, changing, washing my hands, and brushing my teeth afterward. I tossed the pack before it was empty. The effort to be discreet and find a few hidden moments wasn't worth it.

Instead, I spent TJ's unpredictable naps reading about the pros and cons of redshirting and the benefits of full day versus half day kindergarten. But I should have spent less time comparing notes with other moms and researching, and more time listening to my own instincts.

13

DASHED EXPECTATIONS

Jesus said to them, "Let the children come to me, and do not
hinder them, for the kingdom of God belongs to such as these.
Truly I tell you, anyone who will not receive the kingdom of God
like a little child will never enter it." And he took the children
into his arms, placed his hands on them, and blessed them.

—Mark 10:14–16

September 2014

The fourth week of school brought little in the way of change. TJ and
I arrived for lunch duty to find Jack teary again. After my lunch duty,
I wheeled TJ's umbrella stroller into the basement office of the school
social worker. The room was cramped, containing only a small desk
against the wall and a small table with three school chairs. The social
worker looked to be early twenties.

TJ squirmed in the stroller. I handed him a toy which he
promptly tossed. The social worker rummaged in a bin below her
desk and extracted some brightly colored puppets. She handed them
to TJ. He examined them appreciatively. The social worker gestured
to the chairs. I sat stiffly, knowing I had little time before TJ became
restless.

"So tell me, what's been going on?" The social worker tapped a
pen on a white legal pad.

I explained Jack's anxieties, how he had trouble sleeping worrying about school, and his struggles with lunch and long days. She nodded, scribbling on her legal pad.

"One of the girls in Jack's class gets picked up just before lunch. I think that would be a good option for Jack since he did really well with half days the first week."

The social worker clicked her pen. "Yes, I know that family. They've been with the school a long time. We don't actually offer half days, though." She nodded to herself. "We believe without afternoon enrichment, kids fall behind."

"He's a young five," I said. "He turned five in June. Some boys in his class are already six. That's a big difference at this age, in terms of maturity."

The social worker tapped her pen to her chin and then sat her pen and pad of paper on the table, leaned back, and sighed. "I know it can be hard to let go."

I stared at her. Were we speaking separate languages? I gestured toward TJ. "He keeps me plenty busy. I've actually been really looking forward to spending one-on-one time with him."

"Then why would you want to move Jack to half days?" She raised a penciled eyebrow at me. "That will rob TJ of alone time with you, and that's not really fair, is it?"

I frowned and looked at TJ. I'm often amazed by parents with multiple kids. Even with two, juggling needs constantly left me feeling as though I was falling short.

"Well, we make the most of our time. I give him my undivided attention in the mornings. Typically, though, he naps in the afternoons, *if* we're lucky." I laughed awkwardly, wondering why I felt the need to explain all of this. "It would actually work out really well to bring Jack home at lunch. I could spend time with him while TJ naps. "Plus, I really think he'd do better," I rambled. "The lunchroom is a lot for him."

She pulled her light brown hair out of its ponytail holder. "The lunch ladies aren't seeing what you're seeing. If you've seen him crying during lunch, it's for *your* benefit. Kids are master manipulators. They really know how to pull on our heart strings."

Which you apparently don't have, I thought while she tossed me a patronizing smile. I stopped short of asking her if she'd found her degree at the bottom of a Cracker Jack Box.

"He didn't see me," I said. "I was just coming in, and I saw him sitting there, crying. No one was around to see. The lunch moms are busy, so that might be why they aren't seeing."

"You know, you've been volunteering for lunch duty a lot."

It sounded like an accusation. I realized she was waiting for an explanation.

"I signed up for a few things at orientation. As you know, parents are required to put in twenty volunteer hours per year. You can't bring siblings into the classrooms, so my options are limited with TJ."

"I'm suggesting you don't volunteer for lunch or recess anymore, and certainly nothing inside the classroom—maybe you're around too much."

TJ tossed his toys aside. "Go home!"

"Okay, TJ, we're going." Clearly, I wasn't getting anywhere, and I needed to get TJ home for his nap. I got to my feet, practically shaking with frustration.

"I have to bounce too," the social worker said. "I'll take the elevator with you."

Oh, great, and here I thought we'd have to end this pleasant interaction, I thought bitterly.

We walked to the elevator in silence. I lifted TJ out of his stroller so he could hit the button. "Hit number one, TJ," I said as we stepped into the small box.

"One." TJ proudly jabbed the button. I set him down, keeping my eyes on him in case he decided to go for the alarm.

"I know it's hard, Mom," the social worker piped up as the creaky elevator began to ascend, "but kids do this, especially during transitions."

That did it. I looked her in the eye. "I have a degree in psychology—you don't need to teach me about child development. And you definitely don't need to teach me about my own son and his needs based on the minute you saw him in the lunchroom."

Her patronizing smile fell, leaving behind an "o" of surprise. The elevator doors opened. I took TJ's hand and navigated the stroller with my free hand. Then I marched out of the elevator, past the front office (ignoring the princess wave of Front Desk Lady), and excited the building, leaving the social worker behind with her mouth hanging open.

14

THE BLUEBIRD OF HAPPINESS

Let no one deceive you with empty words.

—Ephesians 5:6

September 2014

"Good night, Jack. I love you." I turned the light off.

"Mommy? Jack's little voice called out into the darkness, softened by the pale green glow of the night.

I knew the tone. He had something on his mind. These types of revelations often occurred in the quiet moments between bedtime and sleep. I returned to Jack's bedside.

He looked up at me, his eyes inky in the darkness. "Am I a baby?"

"What do you mean? You're a big five-year-old."

"Evelyn said I was a baby."

I pictured the little blond-haired girl who sat next to Jack. "She did? When?"

"Today when I was crying because I didn't want you to leave. Mrs. TwentyfiveYearsExperience took me in the room, and when I sat down Evelyn said I was a baby 'cause big boys don't cry and babies can't go to this school." Jack sucked in a breath.

"Did Mrs. TwentyfiveYearsExperience hear?" I asked.

A complicated web of emotions crystallized in my chest. I had a long history of being bullied as a child. It was a big fear I had with sending my kids to school.

Jack shrugged his slender shoulders under the blanket and rubbed his snuggle blankie on his face. "She told Evelyn that was enough. Then Evelyn said snuggle blankie was babyish."

"Is that why you stopped bringing it to school for rest time?"

Every afternoon the kindergarteners had a brief rest time. Parents had purchased blue "rest mats" resembling gym mats at the beginning of the year. Teachers had sent a note home asking parents to send in a small blanket and comfort item for rest time. Jack's snuggle blankie went with him to school each day and arrived home with him every afternoon, safely zipped in his backpack. One day in the middle of the previous week Jack had sadly, reverently removed the tattered cloth from his backpack and put it back on his bed. He hadn't wanted to bring it back to school since. When we asked him why he said he just didn't want to take it anymore.

This was the first time Jack had been made to feel embarrassed about something so precious. I felt this loss of innocence acutely, and I was caught off guard by the intensity of the anger I felt toward this little child. Maybe I'm naïve, but it deeply saddens me that kids learn cruelty so young.

"Jack, you know you can tell Dad and I anything?"

He nodded.

"Your snuggle blankie is *not* babyish. It's incredibly special. Anyway, all of the kids were asked to bring a blanket."

"Yeah, but the other kids' blankets are plain. Snuggle blankie has boats on it."

"What's babyish about boats?"

Jack frowned.

"If it makes you feel better, you can bring the plain orange blanket."

He nodded, looking pensive.

"But you know, there's nothing wrong or babyish about having a comfort item. It's a good thing. Even adults have them."

"Even you?"

"Yep. I still have my stuffed dalmatian, Pepper. I've had him since I was five. I'll show you something else I carried to school, even in high school and college, it was always in my pocket."

I alighted to my own room and retrieved my plastic bluebird. It fit easily in the palm of my hand. The bird's crystal pattern allowed it to catch the light when the sun trickled in from the adjacent window. I brought it back to Jack's room. I sat on the bed and held the bird up in the light of the nightlight.

"This bird is called the bluebird of happiness. My dad gave it to me when I was in seventh grade, when I was having a really tough time in school." My father had given me the bluebird of happiness along with a card explaining its significance when I was diagnosed with major depressive disorder at thirteen. "I carried it in the pocket of my skirt. I could reach in and touch it and feel better. I even carried it to job interviews."

Jack studied the bird. "It helps?"

"It helps me. If you want, you could carry it in your pocket or in the small compartment of you backpack. Just for you."

"I'd like that." Jack's lids fluttered.

"Would you like me to talk to Mrs. TwentyfiveYearsExperience about what Evelyn said?"

"Will she tell Evelyn that I told?"

"No, sweetie, I'm sure she won't. But I won't talk to her unless you tell me to." I wanted Jack to feel comfortable telling me anything.

"I want you to talk to her, but I don't want Evelyn to get into trouble. I just want her to not call me names anymore."

"Okay, sweetie. We'll take care of it."

"Okay."

"Get some sleep. Love you."

*****

That night I sent two emails. The first was to Mrs. TwentyfiveYearsExperience asking if I could speak to her briefly about a concern regarding Jack and another student. The second I sent to St. Agnus's principal, Mrs. Favoritism, requesting permission to retrieve Jack before lunch.

The next day Jack announced that a boy had climbed under the stall while he was using the bathroom.

"A boy from your class?" I asked.

"No, he was from the first-grade class. I asked my teacher if I could go to the bathroom during art. He came in while I was in there and put his head under the stall." Jack frowned. "He thought it was funny."

"It wasn't funny," I said. "The bathroom is private." I coaxed more information out of Jack, finally confirming the boy had done nothing more than poke his head under the stall door. I assured Jack I had a meeting with his teacher the following morning after drop-off. "Go in nicely so I can talk to her."

"Okay, I will. The kids didn't laugh at the orange blanket. I missed snuggle blankie, but I had the bluebird of happiness in my pocket and no one even knew!"

I smiled. "Good. You know Jesus goes with you to school every day. You can always talk to Him."

Jack giggled. "I bet His legs get cramped in those little chairs!"

It was good to hear Jack's giggle. I've always loved his high-pitched laugh. That night I relayed the new information to Luke. He shook his head.

"I'm sure it was just a little boy being goofy, but it must've surprised and upset Jack. You're meeting with Mrs. TwentyfiveYearsExperience first thing in the morning, and then Mrs. Favoritism directly after?"

I nodded. The boy was just being silly. Still, after this incident Jack would refuse to use any school or public restroom until well into his preteen years. It's something he struggles with even today, even though he no longer consciously remembers the incident.

"Let's see what the teacher and principal say, but I'm starting to lose faith in the school," Luke said.

"These meetings will help us decide whether to move him to Trinity," I said. My friend Naomi's son had gone to preschool with Jack and attended half-day kindergarten at Trinity Lutheran grade school. The abbreviated 8:20–11:30 program might be a more manageable day for Jack.

We were on the fence about making the change. Luke was concerned yet another transition would only increase Jack's anxiety. Other more seasoned parents had advised us it was too soon to give up on Saint Agnus and full days. Give it at least until Halloween, they said.

Meanwhile, Jack gave no sign of pending adjustment. He cried every night and every morning. Drop off continued to be gut-wrenching. Most days, Jack refused to exit the car. He continually reported asking to go to the nurse's office during lunch, and his lunch and snack came home untouched every afternoon. The most I got from the school was that they'd give Jack a buddy to walk with from lunch to recess, but according to Jack this did not happen. I was not to be placated.

*****

The following morning, Jack reluctantly entered his classroom. While the aid was taking attendance and leading the pledge, Mrs. TwentyfiveYearsExperience stepped out into the hallway to speak with me. She stood with her back to the classroom door as though guarding it.

"Thank you for meeting with me. I won't keep you long," I said.

The teacher gave me a tight-lipped smile. "Of course, Jack is a wonderful boy. I know you have concerns, Mrs. Shepherd, but he really is doing fine."

"He told me Evelyn called him a baby and teased him about his blanket."

Mrs. TwentyfiveYearsExperience glanced up and down the empty hallway like she was hoping to be rescued. "Well, kids say things."

Really? "Well, it really upset him."

"Yes, Jack is a sensitive boy."

Or Evelyn's just a bully, I thought bitterly. "Mrs. TwentyfiveYearsExperience, I appreciate you have eighteen kids, but name-calling is a form of bullying. I know Saint Agnus has a strict anti-bullying policy."

The teacher's lips formed a thin line. "Evelyn was spoken to."

"That's great. I'll ask Jack if it's still happening. Also, apparently a boy, maybe a first grader, poked his head under the bathroom stall while Jack was in there. It was during art."

The teacher sighed. "Yes, I do allow students to use the restroom during class if they raise their hands. I can't monitor children from other classes. I'm sorry that happened."

We stared at each other for several moments. I'm not sure what I was hoping to get out of our meeting. "I won't take up anymore of your time. I'm actually meeting with Mrs. Favoritism to discuss Jack attending half-days like Sara."

"Hmm. You can ask her, but honestly, Mrs. Shepherd, Jack does just fine in the afternoons. Specials are the fun classes and I'd hate for Jack to miss out."

"Well, thanks again for your time."

We parted awkwardly. I headed to Mrs. Favoritism's office, where I had an equally "productive" meeting.

"Mrs. TwentyfiveYearsExperience and the social worker informed me you had questions about half-days. We don't offer half-days here at Saint Agnus." She nodded, as though the matter was resolved, but I was just getting started.

"I know you don't. But I figure I can pick Jack up when the kids are heading to lunch, like Sara's mom does. That way, it won't be disruptive. We're not asking for a discount in tuition or anything. We'll still pay full price."

"See, the thing is that family has a special arrangement with the school." She blinked her spider lashes. Was that supposed to be meaningful to me? I found out later the "special arrangement" meant the family donated large sums of money to the school.

"Well," I said after a beat of charged silence, "Maybe we can have a special arrangement with the school? I mean, we've been parishioners at the church for six years. I even run the mom's group here. Jack could do half-days this year, and then we could assess whether he's ready to move on to first grade."

"Jack is ready, academically. His placement exam over the summer showed as much. In fact, Mrs. TwentyfiveYearsExperience says he's the most advanced student in her class."

"If I could just pick him up before lunch. He's a young five, and socially—"

"He's not the only young five, Mrs. Shepherd. All due respect, no one at this school has any concerns about Jack. We wouldn't recommend half days."

"Well, that's what Luke and I would like to do. We feel it's best."

Mrs. Favoritism gave her head a quick shake, resembling a wet dog. "I'm afraid that's not possible."

It was possible, obviously. Another family was doing it. But it would do no good to point out this hypocrisy.

"Then I guess we're done here." I got to my feet.

Mrs. Favoritism rose as well. "Thanks for coming in."

I glanced at the *Catholic School Pride* banner hanging above her head and then locked eyes with Mrs. Favoritism. "This will be Jack's last week at Saint Agnus. We'll be expecting a full refund of October's tuition, as well as the registration fee and technology fee."

It was the first and last time I'd interact with Mrs. Favoritism. We were done.

15

Kindergarten, Take 2

I can do all things through Him who gives me strength.
—Philippians 4:13

October 2014

My friend Naomi lived down the block from Trinity Lutheran Elementary. We were meeting at the school playground at seven thirty on a crisp fall morning to celebrate Jack's first day at Trinity. The school was small and only had one kindergarten class, ensuring Jack would be in class with his friend and Naomi's son, Xander, just like he had in preschool.

"Hey, hey, hey, ready for your first day? The amigos together again," Naomi called as Jack hopped out of the car and dashed toward the mulch as though fueled by the scent of the doughnut holes supplied by Naomi.

Excited chatter floated to me as I unbuckled TJ's car seat and searched the car floor for his other shoe. My back pain had been flaring up lately, and my spine protested as I lifted TJ onto my hip and hoisted the diaper bag over my other shoulder. I wandered over to where Naomi was standing at the edge of a small playground handing out doughnut holes from a box set on the wrought-iron bench next to her.

"You're a hot mess, girl," she said, giving me a one-armed hug.

TJ shimmied down my body and dove for the doughnuts. Naomi intercepted him and handed him two chocolate munchkins. I looked at the bench and smiled. A poster declaring WELCOME TO TRINITY, JACK! sat propped up on it.

"Jack, did you see the nice poster Xander made for you?" I called to Jack, who was traversing a modest climbing structure with Xander and his little brother, Drew.

Jack smiled down at me, his mouth outlined with powdered sugar. "Uh-huh. Xander and I will be in the same class.

"Noah is in Ms. Sheridan's class too," Naomi said. "The three of you will be in class together, just like in preschool. The kids played until the first bell rang. "Usually, we pull around to that door and let the kids out," Naomi told me. "But they'll let you walk him in."

Naomi and I both walked our boys in that day. We got a picture of Jack, Xander, and their friend, Noah standing outside the classroom with the teacher—an updated first day of school picture.

"Show him around. Introduce him to the other kids," Naomi called as Xander took Jack by the hand and led him into the classroom.

"We're happy to have Jack," Ms. Sheridan, a slight young woman with cropped brown hair assured me.

"Come on, he's good. Xander's got him. Let's go back to my house and finish our coffee."

"Bye, Jack," I called. I followed Naomi back out to the parking lot.

Back at Naomi's house, Drew and TJ played trains in the basement while she and I sat on the cream-colored carpet nearby and talked. I filled Naomi in on Saint Agnus and feeling like I was treated like some overbearing mother.

"The mama gut always knows." She nodded sagely.

My heart swelled with gratitude. When it feels like a number of people are standing against you, it's a relief to be reminded who is in your corner. "Thank you for today."

"Your life is going to be a lot easier now," she answered.

*****

Jack was still nervous to attend school, but he was comforted by Xander's presence. He would not exit the car without physical prompts from me. Fortunately, the friendly principal standing outside kindly waved me into one of the parking spots adjacent to the playground, where I could park long enough to walk Jack to his classroom.

Each morning I'd siphon through the drop-off lane, park in what quickly became "my" spot, unbuckle Jack's five-point harness, and set him on the blacktop. Once I'd draped his backpack on his slender shoulders, I took his hand and walked over to the driver's side to unbuckle TJ and pop him onto my hip or into the baby carrier strapped to my chest, which we still used sometimes when I really had my hands full. Jack's classroom was a mere twenty feet from the door, but I was typically sweating by the time I deposited Jack at the doorway of the brightly colored classroom.

The mother of a cute little blond girl in Jack's class had five young children, two of whom were younger than kindergarten age. Watching the slender young mother usher all of her children from her car to the building each morning, I couldn't help feeling a little inferior. She made it look so easy with five, while I was sweating and struggling with two. Though I'm still not immune to it, I've since learned the futility of comparison.

"How was your school day, Jack?" I asked one day when I picked him up.

"Bad," he replied with zero inflection in his voice.

"Really? Why? What happened?"

"I spilled my apple sauce pouch at snack. Never give me apple sauce again."

I sighed, mentally listing alternative healthy but less messy snacks. "Okay, what happened when you spilled your apple sauce?"

"Ms. Sheridan gave me some napkins, and I cleaned it up. She wasn't mad."

I carefully pulled out of the lot. "That's good. Everyone spills things sometimes, even adults." I paused, thinking of the little girl at St. Agnus who'd called Jack a baby. "Did anyone say anything when you spilled the applesauce?"

"Nope."

"Okay, so what else happened in your day?"

Jack let out the exasperated sigh of a child asked one too many questions by a parent. "Well, let's see. Xander, Noah, and I played tag at recess, and I won. Then Ms. Sheridan gave me a blue star for reading, and I also got to pick a prize from the prize jar. I picked a car for TJ. Here you go, TJ."

I glanced in the rearview in time to see Jack hand TJ a blue car. I smiled at the sweet gesture.

"Ohh, thanks," TJ said.

"That was nice of you to think of your brother, Jack. I'm proud of your sticker. What did you get to pick a prize for?"

"Good behavior."

"So wow, a star for reading, and a champion at tag. Sounds like a good day besides the apple sauce."

"I guess."

"You know, sometimes bad things happen on otherwise good days. It doesn't mean the whole day was bad."

"I know."

In the past two years, Jack had developed a glass-half-empty view of the world. If a single not-so-great thing happened in an otherwise good day, the whole day was bad in Jack's eyes. I treaded carefully, dodging the temptation of invalidating feelings with a dissertation on attitude.

I learned to ask Jack what the good parts of his day were. What was the best part and what was the worst? Or as Naomi put it, what was the pit and what was the peak? Jack's answer was always the same. The pit was going to school and the peak was leaving school. He liked Trinity better than St. Agnus, he said. Mornings were still a struggle but worries about school no longer monopolized his time at home, so that was something.

Once or twice a week we'd make the five-minute drive to Naomi's house for lunch. I cherished those afternoons. The boys played while Naomi and I talked and sipped La Croix. One sunny day, the boys rolled out construction paper and drew while Naomi scoured her cabinets.

"Tuna for us and mac and cheese for the boys?" she asked, pulling cans and boxes from her pantry.

I nodded from my stool at her counter. "Need help?"

"No, girl, you stay there. Will your boys eat cucumbers?"

"Jack will. TJ, not so much."

She nodded. "Drew will only eat them if they're cut length-wise instead of in circles." She rolled her eyes.

Jack and Xander wandered into the kitchen to check on the lunch progress. Naomi cracked the can of tuna and dumped its contents into a bowl. Jack suddenly looked at me, his face ashen and his blue eyes panicked.

"What's wrong, Jack?" I vacated my chair.

"The smell..." He put his hand over his mouth and bolted for the front door, letting himself out into the fresh air. The door slammed shut behind him.

Naomi and I looked at each other. "The tuna?" she inquired.

"He's been extremely sensitive to smells and loud noises," I said as I headed for the front door. "He never used to be. It doesn't smell that strong to me."

I found Jack on the front stoop doubled over, gagging. I put a hand on his back.

"I'm sorry, Jack. The tuna smell was too strong?"

"I feel like I'm gonna throw up," Jack moaned.

"Okay, why don't you stay in the fresh air for a few more minutes? Mrs. Jenkins and I will take our sandwiches out on the back porch, so you won't have to smell the tuna. You guys will sit at the dining room table. She's making you mac and cheese."

Jack glared at me. "How can you eat that stuff? It's so disgusting."

I shrugged. "A lot of people don't like it, but I always have."

Naomi appeared in the doorway, propping the storm door open with her arm. "The coast is clear." She offered Jack a thumbs-up sign. "I brought the sandwiches out on the back porch and lit a candle. The mac and cheese is ready."

Jack eyed her suspiciously, but the promise of his favorite lunch was enough to lure him back inside.

"Thank you," I mouthed to Naomi.

Jack sniffed the air like a bloodhound attempting to detect a scent.

"Does it smell better in here?" Naomi asked.

Jack nodded vehemently. "Yes, much better thanks."

Like usual, Naomi and I planned to enjoy our lunch on the screened-in porch while the boys ate at the dining room table. When I helped Naomi carry the four plates to the table, Jack looked at his brother and friends before picking up his plate and retreating to the kitchen.

"Jack, where are you going?" Xander called. "Come back and eat with us."

"I can't," Jack called back over his shoulder. "I can't eat next to other people."

"Yes, you can! You always do. You did last time."

Xander was right; this behavior was new.

"Mom, I want to eat outside with you."

"We've got the tuna outside, bud," Naomi said. "Go sit at the kids' table with your friends and let your mom and I eat."

One look at Jack told me when he said he couldn't eat by the other kids he absolutely *could not*. He settled for eating at the counter by himself. He insisted that I stay inside with him despite the fact that the door to the porch was off the kitchen, and he could see me from his seat. I spent the remainder of lunch dashing out to the porch to steal bites of my sandwich, and back in to check on Jack and TJ. Jack never took his eyes off me, and no amount of coaxing from Xander convinced him to return to the table where he'd sat during our previous visit.

When was it? He'd had a cold the previous week, so it had been at least two weeks. Now, out of nowhere, he couldn't eat lunch by his friends, or even his brother.

At home, he began bringing his plate into the dining room to eat in solitude, abandoning his customary spot at the kitchen table with the rest of the family. Dinner as a family was so important to me. Growing up, family dinners—television off—were mandatory. If we attempted to force Jack to eat with us, he became agitated and then hysterical. He'd scream, cry, clear his throat, and gag. On one occasion, he even overturned a full plate of food in a fit of rage. If one of us offered him company he'd silently pick up his plate and walk off in search of a private location—if he didn't stop eating entirely.

I had to be careful what I introduced in terms of cleaners, candles, or cooking. I used gentle, all-natural cleaners. I allowed Jack to sit alone to eat. If we had family get togethers I had to request that guests not go and sit next to Jack while he was eating, asking confused grandparents not to encourage him to sit with us.

He continued to struggle with separation at home and going to school. At home, he was afraid to go upstairs or even in the other room without one of us. He needed me to lay next to him to fall asleep at night. He had intrusive thoughts of people breaking in his second-story window to kidnap him. He saw people in the shadows. Typically, it took him upward of two hours to fall asleep. As an infant, Jack had been a champion sleeper.

The drop-off procedure at school had become increasingly arduous. I was parking and carrying him into the building, wrangling TJ while Jack grabbed for door frames. Then I would deposit Jack into the arms of his kind, supportive teacher. Meanwhile, TJ made his way into the adjacent preschool room. I told Jack "goodbye" and "I love you," and dashed after TJ, who protested vehemently when I pried toys out of his hands and carried him back out to the car. More often than I'd like to admit, I cried exhausted tears the whole way home. Although the staff at Trinity were nothing but kind and did all they could to help, those mornings were emotionally taxing on both Jack and me.

Though his teacher assured me he was fine throughout the morning and socialized well with the other kids, he brought the majority of his in-class worksheets home blank. When I asked him why, his answer was a sieve around my heart. "I missed you too much."

I sat down at the kitchen table to complete the work with him, and he flew through it. Halloween came and went. The leaves changed from green to gold and burnt orange before shivering off the trees. Still, Jack struggled with what we later learned was called "school refusal." We decided to take him to a child psychologist.

16

STRIP-MALL PSYCHOLOGIST

Those who look to Him for help will be radiant with
joy. No shadow of shame will darken their faces.

—Psalm 34:5

November 2014

Dr. Old School was a spindly man with snow-white hair and wire-
rimmed glasses. He wore cardigans over button down shirts and khakis. During our initial phone consult I outlined Jack's anxieties, his
difficulty eating around others, his sensitivity to sounds and smells,
and his resistance to school. He got us in for an appointment within
the week.

"I'm taking you to see a psychologist," I told Jack. "That's a
doctor you can talk to about any worries, thoughts, or feelings you
might have. I've seen psychologists or counselors at different times in
my life and found it helpful."

"Will I have to get a shot?" Jack asked.

"No. No shots."

"Okay, then I'll go. You have to go in with me."

I hesitated. Dr. Old School and I had discussed this. "I'll go in
with you initially, but then I think Dr. Old School wants to talk to
just you and maybe play some games with you. TJ and I will be right
outside the door in the waiting room."

"Well, I'm not sure how I feel about that," Jack said, his pout contrasting with his mature speech.

"Let's see how it goes. It won't be long—under an hour." My first mission was to simply get Jack there. I never knew how he'd react to a new situation or activity.

Dr. Old School's office was a small space at the corner end of a modest strip mall. The sparsely decorated waiting room contained tattered black chairs arranged in a square, in the middle of which sat a wood coffee table littered with magazines. A lone tree stood sentry near the door. I immediately had to save the defenseless tree from TJ's curious hands.

The interior of Dr. Old School's office was painted a cool green and adorned with a black leather couch kitty corned to a stuffed chair. An oversized oak desk crowded the far corner. Dr. Old School gave TJ a plastic school bus and some little people. Jack flopped on the couch, and I perched next to him.

"Thanks for the toys," I said. TJ loves school buses. Shoes, not so much." I smiled nervously, indicating TJ's sock-clad feet. He'd begun taking his shoes off in the car. They were stashed in my diaper bag.

"Yes, well, if you enforce it he'll wear them."

I frowned. Enforcing my two-year-old's compliance with shoes was not at the top of my priority list. I'm a firm believer in picking my battles.

"Do you like school, Jack?" the doctor began.

"No."

"No?" the doctor feigned surprise. "Why not?"

"It's boring, and I have to leave Mom."

"But you know your mom always comes back."

"Yeah…"

"Do you have friends at school, Jack?"

Jack shrugged.

"One of his best friends from preschool is in his class," I offered.

"Please don't touch anything over there," Dr. Old School said.

I retrieved TJ who had wandered over to the desk. He protested vehemently.

"It's okay to say no, Mom," Dr. Old School said.

"I know. It's just, he's two, so he's still in that exploring phase." I handed TJ a blue and orange Hot Wheels car. I was beginning to sweat, getting the itchy feeling of being under a microscope.

"Jack, how about your mom and brother wait outside the door while you and I talk and build?"

Jack looked at me and shook his head.

Dr. Old School rose and began rummaging in his closet. He extracted a Kinex set. Jack watched him warily. "You and I are going to build this while your mom and brother wait in the waiting room, just outside that door." He pointed.

"We'll be right outside, Jack." I gathered up TJ and the toys. Jack glowered at me but didn't protest when I exited the office and shut the door behind us.

*****

Dr. Old School firmly coaxed Jack into the office each week while I tried to contain TJ in the waiting room with books and toys. Jack wasn't fighting going to sessions, but he wasn't making any progress either.

Luke and I scheduled a feedback session with Dr. Old School to touch base. I hadn't gotten much feedback from him and I was anxious to hear his thoughts. Jack said Dr. Old School was nice, and he liked building with him, but that was the extent of my insight.

We scheduled the appointment for 8:00 PM so that Luke could make it. My mom came over to watch the boys. Dr. Old School opened the door wearing a forest green cardigan. He shook Luke's hand.

"It's nice to meet you. Thank you for meeting with us," Luke said.

Dr. Old School parked in the chair while Luke and I took our places on the couch. This was the first time we'd sit in a therapist's office to discuss our son, but it would be far from the last.

"So," Dr. Old School began, "why did you want to schedule this meeting?"

I frowned, confused by the question. Why wouldn't we want his insights on Jack?

"We want to hear your thoughts on what's going on with Jack and how he's doing," Luke said.

Dr. Old School clasped his hands over his knee. "For starters, Jack is an extremely bright boy. He plays well with me and asks many intelligent questions—questions you wouldn't expect from a five-year-old. For example, he was looking at my smoke detector." He gestured toward the small white box on the ceiling. "He asked me all about the system, how it was wired up, how it worked, if it was connected to the other smoke detectors in the strip mall... Most five-year-olds wouldn't even notice something like that."

Luke beamed. "Yes, Jack is very observant and inquisitive. He always has been."

"Jack also has a lot of worries," the doctor continued. "He tells me he has friends he plays with at morning recess, but he doesn't like school because"—he consulted a yellow legal pad—"he doesn't like to be away from Mom." He frowned at me. "What's his relationship like with you at home, Mom? It seems he has difficulty separating from you."

I nodded. "Yes, he gets upset even if I'm in a different room."

"You're always home with him?"

"Yes."

He made a note. "What types of activities does Jack engage in at home?"

"His favorite thing is pretend play with me. He struggles to break out of our pretend world and transition to another activity. If I so much as walk away for a drink of water he gets upset."

Dr Old School raised his eyebrows and looked at Luke. "I'm worried Mom is so much fun and so involved that she's fulfilling all of the friendship needs."

"Jack really cherishes Hope." Luke smiled at me. "She plays more than any mother I've ever seen."

"Hmm, yes, well, we just want to make sure she's not taking the place of interactions with children Jack's own age."

"He has friends," I interjected, done with being spoken about as though I wasn't in the room. "Did he tell you about Xander? They've been friends since preschool. And Owen and Brooklyn."

"Yes, he did tell me about his friends. He is a social boy." He paused. "I guess what I'm getting at is, given the choice, would he prefer to go to a friend's house or stay home and play with you?"

I considered this. Jack was fine with going to Xander's house after school as long as I was there. If we were home, he resisted going to friends' houses, preferring for them to come to us.

"He prefers for his friends to come over," I answered.

"But given the choice to play with you or a friend, whom would he choose?"

"Probably me."

"That's my concern. Try backing off on the play."

I frowned. "Jack plays with TJ sometimes, but it doesn't last long, given the age difference. He tends to act out when nothing's going on, and I try to limit screen time, but—"

"Yes, giving in to screen time to entertain isn't a good idea," Dr. Old School said. "Let me ask you this. Do you always stay at playdates, or do you sometimes drop him off?"

"I usually stay."

"Hope is friends with the moms, so it gives her some adult company," Luke offered.

Dr. Old School nodded. "What happens if you drop him off?"

I cringed, thinking of when I'd left him at Naomi's. Naomi and I liked to trade errands. One of us would stay with the four kids while the other ran to the store, and then we'd trade off. Jack would try to prevent me from getting out the door, and although Naomi was quick to swoop in, and I knew he was in good hands, I never felt the errand was worth it.

"He doesn't like for me to leave," I told Dr. Old School. "He hangs on to me and cries."

"Do you linger, or do you leave quickly?"

"As quickly as I can."

"Don't make a production of leaving. When you do that, you make him feel more insecure. Simply say, 'Bye, Jack, I'll be back soon,' then leave, okay?"

I nodded, wondering if that wasn't what I was already doing.

"Now, let's move on to his anxiety. We want a five-year-old to be ready to take on the world. It seems Jack has a lot of fears, many revolving around being away from Mom. We want him to break away from Mom a bit more and gain a stronger sense of self. He also worries about getting hurt or sick, a robber breaking in, fires, and storms." He turned back to me. "Now, Mom, do you get anxious?"

I picked at a cuticle. "Well, I mean, depression and anxiety run in my family, on my mom's side. I struggle with both depression and anxiety, but I wouldn't say I'm outwardly anxious."

"What about storms? How do you react to storms? Do the kids hear you sort of fretting when a storm is coming?"

"No, I've never been worried about storms. I used to actually watch storms with my dad."

"What about other things? Kids can pick up on the anxiety temperature in the room, even when it's subtle."

"Hope doesn't project her worries onto the kids." Luke squeezed my hand. "In fact, she's very calm. She worries most about being a good mother, but you'd never know she's worrying."

"I worry about depression and anxiety in Jack," I said, "since it runs in my family."

"It is genetic," Dr. Old School said.

*****

"It's my fault," I lamented to Luke on the drive home.

"He didn't say that, hunny." Luke patted my thigh. "Even if he had, it's in no way your fault. You're the best mother the boys could ask for."

My mom also tried to reassure me when I arrived home, teary-eyed. I'd already received a loud message, first from Saint Agnus and now from a child psychologist. A little voice inside me was growing louder and louder. The voice said, *it's your fault*. I had to learn to fix things for Jack; how to be the mom he needed. The voice echoed in my head day and night with no reprieve. I threw myself into Jack's therapy, determined to learn as much as I could. Looking back, I should've been learning to trust my own instincts.

17

❧❧❧

SCHOOL REFUSAL

Whether you turn to the right or to the left, your ears will hear
a voice behind you saying, "This is the way. Walk in it."
—Isaiah 30:21

Spring 2015

As the days, weeks, and months passed, I continued to carry, coax,
and cajole Jack into school and complete his schooling at home in
the afternoons. I began researching school refusal. School refusal
describes the behavior of a child who refuses to go to school on a regular basis or has problems staying in school (ada.org). The description fit Jack. Symptoms include headaches, stomachaches, tantrums,
inflexibility, separation anxiety, avoidance, and defiance. Physical
symptoms typically appear before or during school. School refusal
is anxiety-based and not a simple discipline issue. All of my research
suggested exposure. I wasn't so sure.

When I prayed, homeschooling kept entering my mind. True,
I was completing most of Jack's schoolwork with him at home. I was
ordering books and adding my own hands-on activities to keep him
engaged. Nonetheless, the voice of doubt told me I wasn't qualified
to homeschool. I have ADHD, I'm unorganized, and I can't even
keep track of sending birthday cards on time. The voice of doubt

attempted to drown out the voice of truth as I got on my knees each night. After all, homeschooling had never been on my radar.

I asked around about it. I was advised against it. Family worried Jack would miss out on socialization. Luke felt Jack needed to be in a classroom setting, and worried about me balancing homeschooling with giving TJ adequate attention.

"That would just be enabling him," Dr. Old School said when I broached the topic. "Don't give in."

Thoughts of homeschooling continued to nag at me, but I was scared. If I'm being honest, I really didn't want to homeschool. I wasn't comfortable with God's answer, so I was looking for answers elsewhere. But God doesn't give up on us, hard though our hearts may be.

It was important to my mom that Jack attend Catholic school as my brother and I had. Willing to explore every possible option, I agreed when she set up a meeting for Jack and me with the director at the Catholic school attended by my cousin's three children. She happily watched TJ for said meeting.

Jack and I met the director in the gray and white front office. She wore a brown jumper and her blond hair landed just above her shoulders. I'd spoken to her on the phone, briefly describing Jack's school troubles.

"Mrs. Shepherd, so nice to meet you. I'm Sally Sales. You must be Jack."

Jack tentatively took her outstretched hand.

Mrs. Sales chatted proudly about the school as she showed us the classrooms, an art room, the wide hallways, and the large gym. The school was vast and, I thought, a little overwhelming.

"Hi, Dominik," Mrs. Sales said brightly as a boy wearing noise-cancelling headphones passed us in the hallway. He was holding the hand of a young man wearing a lanyard.

Mrs. Sales turned back to us, all smiles. "You see, we have special needs kids here and we're happy to have them. They just need to bring an aid."

She turned around before she could see my mouth drop open. Had she really just pointed out "a special-needs kid"? Maybe it had just come out wrong.

Classes changed and boys in white shirts and khakis and girls in plaid jumpers filtered around us. I smiled. I chatted with Mrs. Sales. I asked questions. "Isn't this nice, Jack?"

I wanted to like the school. I knew how important it was to my mom. I knew it was what Luke wanted. I thought it was what I wanted too, but I wasn't so sure.

On the ride home, Jack had little to say. I set up a shadow day for Jack. Luke would drop him off at seven thirty for the start of the school day, and he would shadow my cousin's kindergartner until I picked him up at lunchtime. Luke called while I was feeding TJ bananas and cheerios.

"How'd he do going in?" I asked. It had become a common question.

"The woman, Mrs. Sales, met us at the front office. She walked Jack to Annie's class. He seemed nervous, but he went with her. I think he felt better knowing that he'd be with Annie."

"Yeah, I hope it works out."

"If it's the best place, we'll make it work."

Was it the best place? I didn't have a good feeling, but maybe I'd have more clarity after Jack's shadow day. When I picked Jack up, he was tired, hungry, and cranky. "What did you think?" I asked him.

"It was fine."

"Did you like it?" I persisted.

"No."

"What didn't you like about it?"

"Everything."

I navigated a wave of frustration. I took for granted Jack's typical open and inquisitive demeanor. "Come on, Bean. Give me an example."

"Fine. It was long and there were too many kids."

"It is a big school. What was good about it?"

"Annie was nice and the teacher was nice, but I don't want to go to school here. Now, can you please stop asking me questions?"

"Sure, I'm just trying to determine the best school for you next year."

"I don't want to go to any school. I just want to stay home with you."

"I know, Jack, but you have to go to school."

But he could stay home with you and still get an education.

My mom was characteristically full of questions when we arrived home. Her expression was hopeful. Jack gave her the same details, or lack thereof, that he'd given me. She turned her attention to me. "It sounds like a great place for him, Hope. Your cousin, Ray, is on the board there. His kids just love it. You could request for him to be in the same class as Annie. Oh, Hope, won't you send him there?"

I rubbed my right temple where a tension headache was forming. "I'm not sure yet, Mom. Luke and I need to talk about it further, and I need to pray on it more." My brain felt like mush and not up for this conversation.

"Hope, why wouldn't you send him there? There's nothing like a Catholic education."

I sighed. "Yes, I know, Mom. I'm just not sure if this school is best for Jack. The classes are large, and the days are long."

"But that's all schools," my mom practically shrieked.

"The day starts at seven thirty and doesn't end until three thirty."

"So?"

"So if he struggles to attend from eight twenty to eleven twenty, that'll be a big jump."

"But he'll be in first grade, hun. He'll have to get used to full days, even in public school. What other choice do you have?"

I glanced at Jack who'd wandered into the family room and begun setting up blocks, which TJ promptly knocked over. I lowered my voice. "Homeschooling," I said, immediately wishing I hadn't.

My mom gasped as though I'd suggested giving up on school altogether. "Oh, Hope, don't do it. You're busy enough with TJ. That would be a big mistake. Plus, how would you *ever* get him back into school? Everyone's telling you it's a bad idea."

"I feel like God's telling me to do it."

"I don't think God would tell you that."

I sighed again. "We haven't made any decision yet."

"Please, he needs socialization. Plus, he'll fall behind. I know you're smart, hun, but you're not a teacher." Luke's parents had the same concerns.

After the boys were asleep that night, I brought up homeschooling again with Luke. "I'm reading this really interesting study. They found that kids struggling with school refusal thrived at homeschooling."

Luke cracked open a beer and looked at me. "Right, but don't they have to go to school at some point?"

"Homeschool *is* school. The study concluded that homeschooling removed the anxiety piece and put the children in an environment conducive to their learning."

"I get that. But TJ takes up so much of your time already. I don't want him to feel like he's losing out on your attention."

"A woman in my Bible study at Good Shepherd connected me with the pastor's wife. They homeschool and also have a toddler. She said she sets her little girl up with toys or an activity nearby. She keeps things on hand just for homeschool time. Then when her first grader is working independently, she plays with the toddler."

"I don't know. I know you can do it, but I still feel he needs to be in a classroom. Won't he fall further behind socially?"

"I don't know. I mean, there are a lot of ways to socialize. How much opportunity do they get to socialize during the school day anyway?" I was repeating an argument shared by the pastor's wife. She'd advised me all homeschoolers had to answer the "what about socialization" question semiregularly.

Along with the question of whether I could adequately educate my child came another, more vain consideration. Could I, the eternal people pleaser, handle the naysayers, even when they included my own husband? If I genuinely believed it was what was best for Jack, I decided, I could.

I knelt down and prayed again. My mind ached with indecision. I was terrified I'd do wrong by my son; terrified, as Dr. Old School had implied, I already had. "*God, tell me what to do.*"

I felt the answer more than I heard it. "*I already told you what to do.*"

"But, God, can I do it?"

"Would I ask you to do something you weren't capable of?"

The following day, I approached Luke again.

"You seem to feel very strongly about this," Luke said.

"Believe me, it's not something I want to do. I believe it's something I'm being asked to do."

"If anyone can do it, it's you." Luke regarded me thoughtfully as we took a rare moment on the couch together. "Tell you what. Let's try it for a year. We'll focus on his counseling and anxiety. Then maybe he can go back to school for second grade."

I didn't want to have to change schooling again in another year, but I took the trial period. *If Jack is meant to be homeschooled, it will work, and Luke will see for himself.*

In the moment of decision, I understood another piece of advice the pastor's wife had given me. She'd said making the decision to homeschool is like jumping into the middle of the ocean without a life vest.

Against all advice, we closed our eyes, and we jumped.

18

HOMESCHOOL HAVEN

Train a child in the way he should go, and when
he is old he shall not depart from it.

—Proverbs 22:6

May 2015

Another piece of God's plan unfolded shortly after we'd made our decision. An old work friend with whom I'd recently reconnected informed me about a hybrid school specifically for homeschooled students. Homeschool Haven met twice per week from nine until two in a church building. The teachers helped with the curriculum. Parents taught at home on the remaining days.

I called Homeschool Haven and set up a meeting with the administrator. The church was about a thirty-minute drive from our house. It was off the main road hidden by a grove of trees. I drove past it three times before finding it. The double doors were locked. I shielded my eyes from the glare and peered inside. Jack knocked. "TJ, no!" I cried, narrowly preventing his little hand from making contact with a nearby garbage can. The door opened.

"Well, hello, you must be Jack and Mrs. Shepherd. I'm Hannah. Who's this?" She smiled at TJ, who was wriggling in my arms.

"This is TJ, and I'm Hope." I transferred TJ to my other arm and held out my hand. "I'm so sorry I'm late. I had trouble finding it."

"Oh, no worries! No worries at all. It is a difficult building to find. We're hidden from the street." She smiled, tucking her jet-black hair behind her ears. Her face was impeccably made up, and her green dress complimented her olive skin.

TJ flailed in my arms as I carried him into the building. I set him down, and he immediately made a beeline for a jar of pencils sitting next to a binder on a long folding table. "Leave that, TJ."

Hannah smiled at TJ. "This is where you check your student in. Usually, one of our moms sits here, but she couldn't make it today so I'm filling in. This is where they eat lunch." She led us behind the table to an open area filled with round tables and blue plastic chairs. A set of doors led into a gym where the kids had recess when the weather didn't permit outdoor play. Hannah turned to Jack and knelt down to his level.

"Jack, Mrs. Z teaches the kindergartners, first, and second graders. They're having class right now. Would you like to sit in?"

Jack looked at me and shook his head.

"What if your mom stays with you would that be okay?"

"Okay."

"I'm afraid TJ would be too disruptive," I said, thwarting his efforts to climb on the chairs.

"Oh, well, we have a little block table right outside the classroom. I could sit with him if you're comfortable."

"Oh, thank you."

"Jack, do you want to take the elevator?" Hannah asked.

Jack's blue eyes widened in excitement. "You have an elevator?"

Hannah smiled back at him. "Yep. We usually have students use the stairs, but this is a special tour."

Jack and TJ raced for the small elevator, clamoring for the button. The elevator took us down one level and opened to a softly lit hallway. TJ spotted the red, green, blue, and yellow block table in a small alcove between two doors.

"That's the art room, and this is Mrs. Z's classroom." Hannah knocked on the second door and then opened it.

A tall woman with thick, wavy blond hair turned from the dry erase board on which she was writing. TJ peeked around my legs in the doorway. Jack tentatively entered the room. Half a dozen little faces, all boys except for one girl, turned to regard us curiously. The room was small with three short tables and chairs.

"I'm sorry to interrupt, Mrs. Zolentino," Hannah said.

"No at all," the teacher smiled. "Class, please read independently for a few minutes."

The kids wandered over to a white bookshelf in the far corner of the room and began poking through books. The teacher came over to us and held out her hand. "Hello, I'm Rebecca Zolentino. The kids all call me Mrs. Z."

"I'm Hope. This is Jack."

"It's nice to meet you. What grade are you in, Jack?"

"Kindergarten."

"Ah. So we've got Austin, who's also in kindergarten." She indicated a boy sitting at a table with a book. He smiled and waved. He was the cutest thing, with a mop of blond hair, green eyes, and a few teeth missing from his joyful smile.

"Then we have Stephen and Michael, who are in first, and Isabella, who's in second." She turned back to me. "Hope, will this be your first time homeschooling?"

"Yes. Jack goes to school now, but we've decided to homeschool for first grade. He needs a smaller class. This is perfect." And it was. Once we filled out the registration packet, a weight was lifted. A decision had been made, and I felt it was the right one.

*****

Jack's kindergarten graduation took place in Trinity's modest gym as May was drawing to a close. My mom and Luke's parents sat in the bleachers with us. I turned the volume down on TJ's leap pad and enabled the camera on my phone. I never expected to be one of those moms who got emotional at kindergarten graduation, but when Jack walked into that gym in his button-down shirt and blue paper cap, my heart swelled. I knew what it had taken for him to get through kindergarten, and I was so proud of his resilience.

That's why I had to respond when a friend's husband made a Facebook post ranting about the ridiculousness of celebrating graduations for kindergarteners. I almost never "get into it" on social media. I simply told him not to take that celebration away or scoff at the milestone because you never know people's stories and what it took for some kids (and their parents) to make it through kindergarten. I couldn't have been prouder (or to be honest, more relieved) than if he'd been graduating from college.

19

MORE FIRSTS

Listen, my sons, to a father's instruction; pay
attention and gain understanding.

—Proverbs 4:1

September 2015

I approached the fall with a turbulent mix of excitement and
trepidation. Luke and I had attended parents' orientation night
at Homeschool Haven, dubbed "HH" by the parents. We were
impressed with the curriculum. Jack would be learning zoology, art,
and math as well as music, chapel, Bible, phonics, language arts, and
health/PE. He'd attend Mondays and Thursdays for half days.

God had also orchestrated the boys' schedules for the fall. TJ
would be attending the "young threes" program at Good Shepherd
Preschool at the same time, offering me four kid-free hours per week
for the first time since Jack's birth.

We met a lot of great parents at orientation, including the
mother of the sweet little blond boy in Jack's class. Her name was Elsa,
and she also had three older girls who attended the K–12 program.

The morning of Jack's first day of first grade was warm and
sunny. I made it a point to exude positivity and excitement. I made
Jack a special breakfast of a chocolate chip waffle with a strawberry
nose and mouth and blueberry eyes. My own stomach churned with

anxiety. It didn't help that we were running a few minutes late (as usual).

"I think you're really going to like it at HH, Jack," I chatted on the drive. "Mrs. Z seems really fun and understanding."

Jack, who'd been quiet for the majority of the drive asked, "What if I get bullied?"

My heart wrenched. I was worried about the same thing, in addition to wondering if Jack's school refusal would persist in this more intimate environment. I was reminded of Julia Roberts character's prayer in the movie *The Wonder* when her son, Augie, begins traditional school for the first time. As she watches Augie join the other kids she says, "Please, God, make the kids be nice to him."

"All the kids are required to sign an anti-bullying and behavior contract," I told Jack. "If you have any problems, talk with Mom and Dad and Mrs. Z. And just think, you've already made friends with Austin."

Finally, we arrived. I signed Jack in and hustled TJ along the corridor. When we reached the classroom, Jack put on the breaks.

"Hi, Jack! Come on in!" Mrs. Z said brightly.

Jack stepped into the doorway and scanned the small classroom. I held my breath.

"Take your time," Mrs. Z said. "Everyone feels nervous on the first day—even teachers!"

Jack looked at her. "Even *you?*"

"Oh, yes! Even as long as I've been a teacher at this school, I still get nervous on the first day. But you know what?"

"What?"

"Once I get over the hump, start the day, and get into the routine, I feel better. Plus, I feel proud of myself. Don't you feel proud of yourself for being so brave coming here on the first day?"

Jack shrugged. "I guess."

"It'll be fine. I promise."

I had to turn away as I began to tear up at the kindness of this teacher toward my son. I nearly collided with Austin and his mom, Elsa.

"Nothing like being late on the first day!" Elsa smiled at me.

I quickly composed myself. "Us too."

"You're earlier than us. Mom of the year here forgot to pack snacks, so we had to make a stop at the gas station for granola bars. I'm just here to make the other moms feel better."

I laughed too. I *did* feel better, but not for the reason she was implying. "At least you got granola bars. My kids probably would've insisted on chips."

"Yay, Mom, Jack's here!" Austin said.

"Bye, Mom," Jack said, following Austin into the classroom.

I intercepted TJ as he tried to follow the older boys into the classroom. I'm pretty sure my mouth was hanging open. "Wow, he went right in. I can't believe it. Not even a hug! I've never been so happy to not receive a hug."

"Sometimes they surprise us," Elsa said.

"I'm really grateful Austin is in his class. He's such a sweet boy, and so kind to Jack."

"Aw, thank you. I'm happy they're together too. Hey, are you heading upstairs? There's coffee and doughnuts for the parents."

My stomach turned again. *I should go, though. I don't want to seem anti-social.* "We'll hang out for a little bit. I promised this guy a trip to the park. TJ, want to get a doughnut?"

I pried TJ away from the block table and followed Elsa upstairs. A handful of parents were gathered around tables in the lunchroom with paper plates and cups. True to form, TJ made a beeline for the chocolate frosted doughnuts.

"Just one, TJ. Let Mom help you." I coaxed one of the doughnuts onto a thin paper plate.

I poured a small cup of coffee for myself and navigated through the tables. I smiled at a woman pushing a baby stroller back and forth. Other than TJ and the baby, I didn't spot any other younger siblings.

Elsa shared her story of running late and stopping at the gas station for snacks. The other parents laughed along with her. As it tends to do, the conversation turned to the kids and the new school year.

"Jack's not a rough-and-tumble boy," I put in. "He's cautious and sensitive." I smiled. Jack's sensitivity was one of his most valuable traits. "I just hope he doesn't get bullied. That happened at his previous school, in kindergarten."

"Austin's like that too," Elsa said. "He tends to hang back when play gets rough. Honestly, bullying doesn't happen here. They're pretty on top of it."

I hoped she was right. My nausea was increasing along with TJ's restlessness. "It was nice meeting all of you," I said as we made our exit.

"Park now?" TJ asked as I buckled him into his car seat.

I kissed his forehead. "Yes, sweet boy. Off to the park."

"Bye, Jack," TJ said when we pulled out of the parking lot.

It took less than five minutes to get to the park. I changed TJ into his swim trunks and swim shirt so he could take advantage of the splash pad. He flailed against my attempts to apply sunscreen.

"Come on, TJ, you don't want to get a sunburn."

I swallowed hard and stood on the perimeter of the splash pad. TJ swatted at a fountain of water coming up from the rubber-padded ground. Once TJ was done with the water I dried him off and chased him through the mulch and up and down the slides. The sun wasn't helping my nausea, and neither was my brain. *Is Jack doing okay? Is he scared? Is he still sticking with Austin? How's he getting along with the other kids in his class? Will he want to go back?*

Fortunately, the park was empty when I had to duck behind a bench and be sick, finally releasing the pent-up anxiety. Spent, I took TJ into the church bordering the park.

"Is your play place open?" I asked the smiling white-haired lady at the front desk.

"Sure, go right ahead."

I lead TJ into the small room containing tunnels, a slide, and a ball pit. I spent the remainder of our time sitting on the floor leaning against the wall, grateful for the air conditioning.

When it was time to retrieve Jack, TJ protested leaving the play place. The lady at the front desk offered me a sympathetic smile while I carried my screaming, flailing toddler and his stinky shoes out of the building.

TJ quieted down once we returned to the car and headed toward the school, but my thoughts did not. I'd soon find out. Did Jack have a good first day?

20

STOLEN MEMORIES

When his parents saw him, they were astonished. His mother
said to him, "Son, why have you treated us like this? Your
father and I have been anxiously searching for you."

—Luke 2:48

September–October 2015

"How was your first day, Jack?" I was emotionally exhausted. My
head ached. All of that disappeared when Jack answered.

"Good."

"He did great!" Mrs. Z smiled.

I watched Jack and Austin laughing and talking. Elsa came into
the classroom behind me. "How'd it go?"

"Good, I guess!"

"Mom, can Austin come over?" Jack asked. His cheeks were
rosy.

"Yeah, Mom, can I go to Jack's house? Please?"

Elsa and I looked at each other. "That's fine with me," I said.

"Really? That would work out. The girls have theater today, so
I could pick him up after their practice."

I happily drove home with an extra kid, to the symphony of
excited chatter. You'd think they'd been friends forever.

As the weeks progressed, the friendship between Jack and Austin continued to blossom. We often used seeing Austin as motivation for Jack to go to school in the mornings. Although our struggles getting Jack to school were nowhere near what they used to be, he still needed coaxing going into the classroom. Stomach aches and headaches on school days were not uncommon.

Mrs. Z had a way with Jack. She often used his interests, which had become increasingly obsessive, to coax him into the classroom. She'd impress him with a tidbit of information about Taylor Swift or Kidz Bop or ask him questions about garbage and recycling.

While we shared in Jack's interests, he often talked about the topics as nauseum, and we had to remind him more than once not to lecture people for throwing a water bottle into the garbage.

At home, Jack's behavior was erratic. Meltdowns were a daily occurrence and could last hours. Sometimes they were triggered by being denied something, but more often by schoolwork, a change in plans, or seemingly nothing at all. During these episodes Jack's eyes would glaze over and his pupils would look like saucers. He'd scream and cry. More disturbing was the strange robot/baby voice he'd revert to—and the aggression.

Jack couldn't be reasoned with during these episodes. He was just…gone. Our only option was to get Jack into a confined space like his room, keep him from hurting himself or someone else, or destroying the house. Then it was a matter of waiting it out minute by agonizing minute, sometimes for hours.

I lay awake at night dreading the moment Luke would leave for work. The difficult truth was I didn't want to be alone with Jack. He was six years old and barely fifty pounds, but during rages he'd become freakishly strong and so out of control—so unlike himself—that I was fearful of him. I felt like I couldn't handle my own child. This sensation riddled me with shame.

Even when Jack was himself, I couldn't bask in the relief of his presence. I felt eggshells under my feet with every step. When would I lose him again? It could be at any moment, with no outward provocation. The pediatrician remained unconcerned and weekly sessions with Dr. Old School failed to produce results. We existed in survival mode.

During one episode, Jack, my mom, TJ, and I were in the house. I don't remember what precipitated it. I sat on the floor of the playroom with my back against the door. Jack hefted a miniature blue wooden chair and rammed it into the door over and over again, wood striking wood directly above my head. Eventually, the tempered glass fell from his eyes. He collapsed and crawled into my lap, remorseful.

Another episode came on a Tuesday afternoon while I attempted to help Jack with his spelling.

"Why do I have to learn how to spell? I can just use spell check."

I sighed. "Come on, Bean. You have such an amazing, beautiful brain. Let's get this done."

"No, I don't want to do it! I refuse!"

"Jack, you need to respect me as your teacher. Remember you have your religious education class tonight and afterward we're picking up Owen. Finish your worksheet so you can play with him."

"No!"

We both grew increasingly frustrated. Ultimately, Jack crumpled up the worksheet, threw it down, and stabbed it with a pencil.

"I guess you'll have to hand it in to Mrs. Z like that," I said, knowing Jack hated to disappoint his teacher.

Jack responded by tearing the paper into confetti and tossing it in every direction. He upended his folding chair and zeroed in on a pile of papers on the desk. I was able to stop him before he ripped up the remaining pages.

Thwarted, Jack turned his aggression toward me, swinging his fists wildly. I grabbed him in a bear hug, and we both toppled to the floor. I knew by now my only option was to wait out the storm. My mistake was holding out hope that we could still salvage any part of our plan.

Jack and Owen were taking a religious education class together on Tuesday nights at a local grammar school. They were preparing for their first communion the following year. That particular evening, I was supposed to collect Owen for Adalyn and bring him home with me until she was finished working. It was obvious Jack wouldn't be able to make the class. When Jack deescalated forty-five minutes in, I crossed my fingers I'd be able to fulfill my commitment to Adalyn. After all, Jack loved seeing Owen and he'd been excited about him coming over. I'd figure out how to handle the schoolwork later.

"I'm not going to RE," Jack announced as I led him and TJ down the stairs.

"I know that, Jack." My voice was heavy with exhaustion. "RE is already almost over."

Jack frowned at me as he climbed into the car, his face filled with confusion. "Wait, it is? Why didn't we go then?"

I looked at him. "You know why we didn't go."

He stared blankly back at me.

I strapped TJ into his car seat, my back aching from my struggle with Jack.

"We're going to pick up Owen," I announced, pulling out of the driveway. I was less than halfway down the block when I heard a distinctive *click*. I braked. "Jack, put your seat belt back on right now!"

"No!"

I swiveled my head around. "Right now, Jack. That is extremely dangerous. If we got into an accident, you'd fly out of the car. Now buckle your car seat."

"No."

I glanced at the clock, mentally cursing. "We have to pick up Owen."

Jack kicked the back of my seat. "Go then."

"I can't go because you unbuckled your car seat. Buckle it, please."

Jack kicked the seat and spit. "Go then! Go, go, go!"

TJ began to wail. At the end of my rope and running out of time, I put my phone on speaker and called Luke. I'm not sure what I expected him to do. I just needed him to answer.

"Hello?"

"Hi."

"What's wrong?" His voice raised an octave.

"Jack had a meltdown over schoolwork and ripped up his paper. We missed RE. Now we're in the car trying to go get Owen, but we only made it halfway down the block. He took his belt off and won't put it back on."

"Doesn't he want Owen to come over?"

"I don't know," I said over TJ's cries. "I thought so." I reached into my bag and handed TJ a squishy giraffe.

"Want me to talk to him?"

"You can try. You're on speaker."

"Hi Jack." Luke waited a beat. "What's wrong, bud? Don't you want to see Owen?"

I looked over my shoulder at Jack. His arms were crossed tightly across his chest, which was rising and falling rapidly. His entire body was rigid. He clamped his mouth shut. *What is he so angry about?*

"Jack?" Luke's voice came through the phone.

Silence. Even TJ was quiet.

"Jack, don't give Mom a hard time, okay? Buckle your car seat and go get your friend. You guys made the commitment to go pick him up. You don't want to keep him waiting."

Reasoning with Jack in this state was futile; trying was foolish. Luke knew it. I knew it. We tried anyway.

Jack was so smart and inquisitive. He possessed understanding and wisdom far beyond his age. I could have deep, meaningful conversations with him. It was hard when that was taken away. It was gut-wrenching when Jack was taken away. We were helpless.

I looked at the clock again. "Hunny, I'm going to let you go. I have to call Adalyn and let her know I can't get Owen." I hated to leave her in the lurch, but I saw no way to safely transport Jack. *If I call Adalyn now, she'll still make it on time.*

I turned the car around, crept down the street, pulled back into the garage, and cut the engine. I decided to text Adalyn so Jack wouldn't hear. She responded immediately. She understood. Still, I felt terrible, and completely defeated. By the time I opened Jack's door, his eyes were clear. It was over.

Jack walked into the house, subdued. I made chicken nuggets for dinner. It was all my dwindling energy reserves could produce. I was bone tired.

Yet somehow, I printed another worksheet, and we completed it together. I gave the boys an Epsom salt bath. We all went to bed exhausted.

The following morning Jack came into my room early. "Mom?"

I rubbed the sleep from my eyes. "Yes, sweetie?"

"Why didn't we go to RE last night? And why didn't Owen come over?" His voice was soft and innocent.

I sat up and rubbed my eyes again. I looked at my boy. His face was open and questioning. Something wasn't right with Jack's behavior and sudden shifts, but I didn't want to absolve him of all responsibility. "Jack, you know why we didn't make it to RE or pick up Owen."

Jack scrunched up his face as though trying to recall a memory. "I was doing my schoolwork and then I don't know. I did more schoolwork. We had dinner, bath, prayers, books, and bed. Did we not go because I had too much schoolwork, Mom? I really wanted to play with Owen."

I got out of bed and went to Jack, standing in the doorway in his Minecraft pajamas. *My sweet boy.* I got down to his level. "Jack, don't you remember ripping up your school paper and having a meltdown? Unbuckling your seatbelt in the car?"

Jack grew pale. He slowly shook his head.

My mouth grew dry. The fear was as potent as it had been that first time he'd been taken as the scary realization dawned on me. This wasn't defiance.

Jack had no recollection of his episode.

21

FOUR AND A HALF HOURS

"How long, Lord? Will you forget me forever? How long
will you hide your face from me? How long must I wrestle
with my thoughts and day after day have sorrow in my
heart? How long will my enemy triumph over me?"
—Psalm 13:1–2

October 2015

For the life of me, I can't recall what triggered the rage. I'd come to
call Jack's episodes rages, but the word didn't encompass what happened to Jack—what happened to all of us.

It was a weekday late in the afternoon. Jack tore through the
house, leaving a path of destruction in his wake. I was on his tail as he
ran through the classroom, ripping up papers. Then he dashed downstairs to grab and throw anything within reach. When he lunged for
TJ I grabbed him, hugging his arms to his sides. He threw his body
backward against me, pushing his feet into the tile.

"Jack, Jack! Let's take a deep breath." He'd begun to hyperventilate. "Please calm down so we can talk about what's bothering you."

Jack lunged forward and sank his teeth into my arm. He did little damage through my long sleeve, but my shock gave him a chance
to break free. He ran from the kitchen to the dining room, grabbing

a blue plastic Mickey Mouse chair and hurling it into the kitchen. It landed with a clatter and skidded across the tile.

My own brain was past rational thought. When Jack went for the chair again, I grabbed it, carried it to the back door, and tossed it outside. Jack emitted a scream that threatened to break windows. I prayed the neighbors wouldn't hear. My main goal was to keep us all safe. I put TJ on the couch and turned on *Disney Junior*, crossing my fingers that he'd stay put. When I turned back around Jack had ahold of one of our tall wooden kitchen chairs. If I hadn't seen it with my own eyes, I wouldn't have believed his forty-some pound body was capable.

Like the Incredible Hulk, Jack lifted the heavy chair over his head and launched it clear into the family room. Thankfully, the only thing it hit was the carpet. I grabbed my phone and Jack, who snarled and spit at me. *This is not my son.* Frantic, I called Luke.

"Hi, hun, I'm on a call. Can I—"

"You need to come home!" I said over Jack's screaming.

I heard Luke sigh. "I'll talk to him."

"I hate you! You're mean!" Jack screamed, trying to wrench away from me.

"There's no talking to him, Luke. Do you hear him? This is the worst it's been. It's been going on for"—keeping my grip on Jack, I looked at the clock above my head—"three hours now."

"What triggered it?"

"I don't know. Does it matter at this point? I'm afraid he'll hurt himself or TJ. Or me."

"Put me on speaker."

Clearly Luke didn't comprehend the scope of this rage. But I hit speaker.

"Jack, what's going on, bud?"

I attempted to swallow the bile of resentment. In my mind, Luke had *no idea.* Jack spit at the phone.

"Just come home," I said. "I can't handle this anymore. I don't know what to do." I was near tears.

"I'll see when the next train—"

Jack shrieked and slapped the phone out of my hand. He took off like a missile. I was weary to my bones. I was scared. When would this nightmare end? Should I call someone? Who? These impossible questions rotated in my head for the next hour while I tried to contain Jack and keep TJ safe. It was about all I could do for my three-year-old during those hours.

When Luke arrived home, he surveyed the house in horror. Torn papers were strewn everywhere, amidst toys and blocks. The kitchen chair was overturned on the family room carpet. TJ was lining up cars. I was numb, holding a flailing, snotty Jack on the couch. I looked up at Luke. My own dismay was reflected in his eyes.

Luke took Jack from me and carried him up to his room. Spent, I gathered up TJ and snuggled him on the couch with *Dr. Suess* books, numb to the screaming and banging from upstairs. Waves of guilt washed over me. TJ needed my attention, but I had so little to give. A half hour later, Luke returned downstairs, his face ashen. The episode had lasted four and a half hours.

"He calmed down finally," Luke said. "I don't know how you did it."

"Four and a half hours," I said robotically.

Luke looked at me sitting on the couch. His expression was pained. "What you said before…I think you're right." He raked a hand through his hair and surveyed the destruction around us. Then he nodded. "You're right. We need to get him formally evaluated by a child psychologist."

22

DIAGNOSIS

"Know also that wisdom is like honey for you; if you find it, there
is a future hope for you, and your hope will not be cut off."
—Proverbs 24:14

November 2015

My leg bounced up and down as I looked around the child psychologist's office. The walls were painted a calming, earthy green. The
office was spacious. A bookshelf contained the DSM, various child
development books, and fidget toys. A blue square toy box sat in the
corner. I waited in a surprisingly comfortable office chair facing a
large oak desk. A white noise machine next to the desk played soothing ocean sounds, but it did nothing to quench my anxiety.

The door creaked open and a man in his mid-forties wearing a
blue and white striped button down walked in. "Hi, I'm Dr. Nick.
Sorry for the wait. I'm a little behind today."

"No problem." I smiled, handing him the stack of paperwork
I'd filled out.

Taking a seat across the desk from me, Dr. Nick perused the
papers. He set them on his desk, folded his hands, and looked at me.
"So tell me a little bit about Jack."

Where did I start? I wanted to tell him every amazing thing
about Jack. I also had to illustrate his struggles.

"Jack is six-years-old," I began. "He's incredibly smart—so much so that his peers don't always understand what he's talking about. Sometimes he talks incessantly about his interests, which include garbage trucks, recycling, Kidz Bop, and Taylor Swift. Recently, he discovered Minecraft, which is a little more relatable to kids his age."

I detailed Jack's school refusal and lastly, his rages, aware that no description could capture their magnitude. "It's like he's somewhere else. Often, he doesn't remember."

Dr. Nick nodded. He typed notes, periodically looking up at me. "Okay," he said, "here's what we'll do. I'll have you bring Jack in for three separate sessions, about two hours each, plus breaks. We do a lot of games and puzzles and test his IQ, memory, and attention. More importantly, I'll do a lot of casual talking with him to assess his social skills and mood."

I nodded. "I'm most concerned about his mood. His separation anxiety interferes with his participation in extracurricular activities and even playdates. Also, he recently started saying things like, 'I can't find my joy,' and he mentions being sad a lot. Depression runs in my family. I've struggled with it since early childhood."

"I look forward to meeting Jack," Dr. Nick said as he walked me out.

I left with a headache, but also curiosity and hope. Maybe we were finally on the way to getting some answers.

*****

"So I'm gonna play games and stuff?" Jack kicked the back of my seat as we drove toward Dr. Nick's office.

"Yep. Dr. Nick wants to see how smart you are. It's kind of a cool way to learn more about your brain."

"Is he gonna help me find my joy again?"

"I hope so, Jack. The goal is to get more ideas on how to help you." I smiled when I got him out of the car, but I was certain it didn't reach my eyes. I'd been careful how I framed the psych testing to Jack. I didn't want him to feel like there was something "wrong" with him.

We checked in at the long reception desk and parked in a smaller waiting area off the main one, which contained books, toys, and a small wooden table strewn with coloring books and crayons. Too restless to color, TJ overturned a canvas cube filled with toys, instantly zeroing in on the cars that tumbled out. I'd barely sat down when Dr. Nick walked in.

"Hi, you must be Jack. I'm Dr. Nick. Today we're going to do a few games and puzzles and talk for a bit, then we'll play a really fun computer game."

Jack looked up at him from behind his long eyelashes. "How long will it take?"

"About two hours, but we'll take a break halfway through. You can come back out here by Mom. It looks like she brought some snacks." He nodded toward Jack's Minecraft lunch box. "Ready to head back? Your mom and brother will be right out here."

Jack latched onto my arm.

"It's okay, Jack," I said. "Go with Dr. Nick."

Jack's fingers dug in.

"I'll tell you what," Dr. Nick said, "Why don't we have your mom come back with us for a few minutes. Then she'll come back out here, okay?"

Reluctantly, Jack nodded. We walked back to Dr. Nick's office, Jack gripping my hand and TJ trying to run ahead. Once in the office, Jack let go of my hand and surveyed his surroundings, curiosity outweighing his apprehension. He squatted down to get a closer look at the white noise machine. "What's this?"

"It's a sound machine," Dr. Nick said. "Go ahead, push one of the buttons." Jack hit a button and the ocean waves turned to rain. He hit another button and a fan sound filled the room. Not wanting to be left out, TJ lunged for the machine, cycling through several sounds in rapid succession.

"TJ, no!" Jack shouted.

"It's okay," Dr. Nick said.

"Jack, your brother just wants to try it," I said.

"He's gonna break it. He breaks everything."

"Jack," Dr. Nick said before I could reply, "your mom tells me you know a lot about garbage and recycling."

"Yeah." Jack turned his attention back to Dr. Nick. "Did you know it takes a plastic bottle six million years to decompose in a landfill?"

"I did not know that."

Once he got Jack talking, TJ and I were able to slip out. Jack did well for the majority of that session, and the two following. Dr. Nick told us as much when Luke and I returned for our feedback session a few weeks later.

Dr. Nick handed each of us a stapled packet of papers detailing Jack's test results. My leg bounced up and down. Luke placed his hand on it. "Whatever happens," he'd told me in the car, "it doesn't change anything."

"It's just a roadmap," I said, the sentence becoming somewhat of a mantra.

Dr. Nick went over Jack's results page by page. Jack's IQ score was 123. His executive functioning, though, was on the lower end. The discrepancy wasn't significant enough to warrant an ADHD diagnosis, but Dr. Nick recommended that Jack be tested again in two to three years to rule it out. My head spun.

"Now I want you to turn to the last two pages," Dr. Nick said, flipping his own page. "You'll see where I've made my recommendations and diagnosis."

23

THE AGE OF REASON

And God said, "Let there be light," and God saw the light
was good. And God separated the light from the darkness.
—Genesis 1:3

October 31, 2018

"That's when he was diagnosed with autism," I told Dr. Kovacevic. "He was also diagnosed with generalized anxiety disorder. That's when we started seeing a new counselor, and per the psychologist's recommendation, he started attending a weekly social group."

"I understand why they diagnosed him with autism," Dr. K said, tapping Jack's psych eval. "These kids, they present with signs of autism, OCD, even schizophrenia. However, these symptoms can vary, or even disappear depending on the timing of the testing."

"Yes," I said, "two years later when he was eight, he no longer met the criteria for autism. The anxiety diagnosis remained consistent."

"Hmm, not surprising. These kids can present as autistic," Dr. K said again, "but autism doesn't come and go. You're not autistic on Tuesday and then not on Thursday."

I nodded, relieved that someone was listening. "Exactly. It never completely fit."

"The other difference is autism can't be cured."

Can Jack be cured?

Dr. K handed Jack's psych eval back to me. "Continue, please."

*****

January–June 2016

I wasn't surprised by the autism diagnosis, but something continued to nag at me. Nonetheless, I accepted the diagnosis and pursued the recommended treatment.

We stopped taking Jack to Dr. Old School. Instead, he began play therapy with Lexi, a pretty woman in her twenties with a thin but curvy frame, olive skin, and highlighted auburn hair. I joked that Luke would not be allowed to take Jack to therapy. Lexi worked at the same practice as Dr. Nick. Jack also began attending a weekly social group at the practice. The group was run by a young counselor with curly brown hair. I met with her one on one before Jack began group.

One frigid Wednesday afternoon in December, I took Jack to his third social group session. Jack had been defiant and moody all day, refusing to do schoolwork and dissolving into tears at the slightest provocation. When the time came to leave, Jack reminded me that he hated social group and *would not* go. The standoff was the same every week.

This particular day was no different. Jack unbuckled his car seat on the way. This move always fast-tracked me to my last nerve. Aside from the defiance, I'd read horror stories of kids being ejected from vehicles after unbuckling seat belts.

"Jack," I said though gritted teeth, "put your belt back on right now." I threatened. I pleaded. I reminded Jack of our weekly routine—if he cooperated attending group we'd stop at Chick-Fil-A on the way home for chicken nuggets and fries. By the time he conceded, we were running ten minutes late.

Jack glared at me as we alighted from the car. "I *hate* social group," he said, as though I'd forgotten. "It's dumb and boring."

"Keep an open mind, Jack. Besides, I bet the other kids can learn from you. You're so smart and such a good friend."

I clung to the remaining gossamer thread of my patience as I half led, half dragged Jack down the long hallway of the square building. After what seemed like an eternity, we reached the group room. I knocked. Celeste opened the door.

"Hi, Jack! Come join us."

That was when Jack lost it. He fell to the floor, his legs kicking out. "I'm not going in!"

I caught the surprised, worried looks of the other kids before Celeste partially closed the door. I caught her surprised look too. She knelt down beside Jack and tried to reason with him.

"I'm not going in unless my mom goes in too."

I squeezed my eyes shut momentarily. Separation anxiety was at the root of so much of Jack's behavior. For the millionth time I wondered if it was my fault. For the millionth time my heart ached for Jack. There was no way he wanted to melt down in front of his peers.

"I don't think it's going to work today," I told Celeste.

We were in a small alcove off the hallway outside the room. The alcove contained two desks and chairs. Jack wrapped his fingers around the metal bottom of one of the chairs, screaming at the top of his lungs. TJ spun the other chair in dizzying circles. I wished for the power of teleportation so we could wait this out at home. We were past the point of no return.

Celeste looked at me. "Since he's not safe to drive, why don't we see if we can get him into my office." She gestured toward the door adjacent to the social group room. "Jack, you and your mom and brother are going to hang out in my office. Take some time to calm down. I'll be in as soon as I have group covered." She returned her attention to me. "Hang in there, Mom."

The moment she disappeared into the group room Jack bolted to his feet and took off back down the hallway.

"Jack, stop!" I scooped a protesting TJ under my arm like a football and pursued Jack. Halfway down the hallway I caught ahold of the hood of his coat. Like a ninja, he shed his coat, leaving me with the hanging polyester.

Jack gained speed, ignoring my calls for him to stop. Weighed down by TJ, I didn't catch him until he'd made it to the main waiting area. A dozen eyes looked up from phones as I lunged for Jack. I caught his arm just as he was pushing on the door leading out to the parking lot. My heart was pounding. Sweat dripped down my back.

"Jack, what are you thinking? You can't run out into a parking lot. You know better." I was right, and I was wrong. *Jack* knew better. But Jack had been taken. This child was in total flight or fight mode.

"We're not going anywhere until we sit in Celeste's office and calm down. You're not going to make group today anyway."

"Fine! You're mean!" Jack shook my hand off and stomped back down the hallway.

I breathed a sigh of relief once we made it to Celeste's office and shut the door. While TJ overturned the small canvas cube containing toys, Jack scoured the room, his pupils inky black and the size of dimes. I had to look away despite how achingly familiar the vacantness had become.

When Celeste entered, Jack was beating up pillows, lunging at them with his little fists pumping. I saw Celeste's look of shock and heard her breathe, "Wow." I'd told her, of course, about the rages in detail. Still, nothing compared to witnessing Jack in this state.

After a few failed attempts to reach Jack, Celeste turned to me. "What do you usually do at home when this happens?"

I stared at Jack, numb. "All we can do is keep him and everyone else safe and wait it out. Typically, my husband or I have to barricade ourselves in a room with him until the switch flips."

Used to Jack's rages, TJ played on the floor, oblivious to his brother's punching and flopping. Jack finally exhausted himself and sat up on the couch, bleary-eyed. For a moment, Celeste remained still as though worried any movement might trigger another landslide.

"Jack? Do you want to talk about what happened?"

Jack wiped his eyes on his sleeve and shrugged. "I guess I didn't want to go in to social group."

"How were you feeling?"

Jack looked down into his lap. An observer would expect the answer to be "angry." "Scared," Jack said instead.

"Why were you feeling scared, Jack?"

"I don't know. I guess I didn't want the kids to look at me. We were late, and I didn't want to go in without my mom."

I rewound the tape in my head. Jack's resistance to attending social group had led to us running late. Arriving late had caused his apprehension to build, like a pop bottle being shaken.

"I love how you identified your feelings," Celeste said. "It's understandable that you felt scared. A lot of other kids feel scared too. No matter how scared or mad we are, we need to stay safe. We can't hurt people or break things, right?"

Jack bounced slightly on the couch cushion. "Right."

"Can we try again next week, even if you feel scared?"

Jack shrugged. "Okay."

Celeste offered me another "hang in there" as she walked us out. I suppose she had a new appreciation for what we were dealing with. I also had the inclination she had no idea how to help.

In the months following social group, Jack had ups and downs, and finally, more ups. He mostly made it to social group, under duress. He continued to work with Lexi. Many sessions, he dug in his heels, and I had to go in with him. I would observe my six-year-old with the vocabulary of an adult vocalize only using grunts and communicate by writing on a dry erase board.

We were seeing some results from therapy, though. Jack was learning deescalation strategies from Lexi. Much of the time he was able to recognize when he was becoming over stimulated and ask for breaks. We were so proud when Jack took himself out of the situation and went up to his room to snuggle with his animals and blanket. He'd return once he was calm. Jack preferred to be with just me or alone during these times. Our families were confused when Jack disappeared from family gatherings, but we knew it was progress.

The progress wasn't linear, though. Jack still had rages. In the absence of a trigger, we had little chance to defuse it. Jack's sweet, gentle nature was punctuated by violent outbursts. Once, he knocked

Adalyn's younger daughter, Brooklyn backward off a plastic chair. She was okay, thank God.

Jack's tics continued to develop. He'd speak in a robotic, baby-like voice and clear his throat repeatedly. He clicked his tongue and chewed his sleeve. He hated bright lights, loud noises, and crowds. Yet none of it was consistent. On one occasion we'd go out and he'd ask for his noise cancelling headphones, and on the next he'd ask why I thought he needed them. His tics seemed to come and go in conjunction with his sensitivities and behaviors. We noticed food dyes seemed to exacerbate his symptoms, so we eliminated them.

I read somewhere that seven is the age of reason. As he approached his seventh birthday, Jack had a string of good days that turned into weeks, and then months. We noticed another pattern to Jack's behaviors, tics, and rages. When he was healthy, he'd function typically. When he was recovering from and illness, he would flare. His behaviors would also flare alongside his allergies.

During Jack's seventh birthday party I had the chance to talk to my good friend, Charlotte. Charlotte was somewhat of a mentor to me. We'd met in a church group when our older boys were both toddlers. Her son had been diagnosed with autism at the age of three. It was Charlotte who'd connected me to the Illinois Autism Moms group on Facebook.

"It doesn't make sense," I told Charlotte while kids ran around and between us. "He'll function typically, sometimes for months at a time. I mean his symptoms will completely disappear. Then overnight he'll become a completely different child."

"Well, there are good days and bad for us, but nothing like you're describing. Autism doesn't come and go," Charlotte said.

"Exactly." I looked over to Jack playing contently with other kids in the family room. "Take his money, for example. He has to count it every night before bed. He pulls out this old Pampers box from under his bed and lays all the bills in rows by value. He has to count it all and write the amount on this scrap of paper, even though it doesn't change. If he's interrupted, he has to start all over."

"And if you didn't let him do it, he'd have a meltdown," Charlotte said knowingly.

I nodded. "Right. Except one night he won't need to count his money anymore. He hasn't counted it for the last three weeks."

Charlotte's eyes travelled over to Jack before she turned her attention back to me. Her green eyes were serious. "You know, that doesn't sound like autism to me. What you're describing sounds like PANDAS."

24

TJ

Children are a gift from the Lord, the fruit of the womb a reward.
—Psalm 127:3

Up until now, this has been about our journey with Jack. TJ's journey is no less important, though less confusing. TJ never left us; he never became someone else entirely. Although many autism parents can pinpoint a point at which their child regressed, I believe TJ had special needs from day one.

I had an uncanny connection with TJ from the moment of his conception. While it might sound far-fetched, I swear I knew the moment TJ was conceived. When the pregnancy test came back negative a few weeks later, I knew the truth. When the test came back positive a couple days later, I wasn't surprised. In utero, TJ was an active baby—so much so that he knocked one of my ribs out of place! TJ was what you'd call a "high needs" baby. He cried and nursed around the clock. It wasn't just crying; he screamed, often for hours on end. The first time he slept longer than a ninety-minute stretch he was fifteen months old. With an on-the-go preschooler, I had no choice but to go about our day with a squalling infant in tow. I myself was a zombie. Naomi does a spot-on impression of me the first time we met in the preschool hallway. I could be found bleary-eyed with unbrushed hair, pushing a stroller with a running soundtrack of screaming.

At night, I'd walk the floors with TJ, pacing an endless circle from the kitchen to the living room and back around. I'd watch the minutes and hours tick by, hungry for sleep. Luke tried to relieve me, but TJ wouldn't take a bottle no matter what kind we tried.

Sometimes he'd sleep in his swing, which swung side to side instead of back and forth. More often, he'd only sleep in my arms as I walked the floors. If I stopped moving, he started screaming. Nursing helped. So did touch. He loved rubbing his hand up and down my arm while nursing. He loved being rocked and carried in the baby carrier. TJ has always been my snuggle bug.

As TJ grew his personality blossomed. He's a sweet, smart, silly boy with tons of energy. He loves animals just like his mom, and outer space, states, and capitals. He's a math whiz, and he has an active imagination.

We also spotted some red flags as he developed, though nothing overly alarming—nothing like Jack's episodes. His motor skills were on the later end. He struggled to develop his "pincher grasp." He crawled with one knee on the floor and the other foot propelling him forward. He walked at sixteen months. This was all still within the normal range.

TJ was two and a half when he began the "young threes" program at Good Shepherd Preschool. Each fall the school brought in an occupational therapist and a speech therapist to observe the kids. TJ was flagged for some speech concerns and some sensory-seeking behavior. Certain sound blends were difficult to understand. Again, at two and a half this wasn't overly concerning. More importantly, though, he didn't engage with his peers at all and often didn't respond to his name or other verbal cues.

We wondered if he had some sensory or auditory processing difficulties. We had TJ evaluated by an occupational therapist. The place was cheery with brightly colored toys and bright green trees painted on the walls. I had the opportunity to observe the evaluation through a two-way mirror.

The occupational therapist was a rosy older woman with short white hair. She positioned TJ on his stomach on a flat swing. As he swung back and forth, she held out brightly colored bean bags for him to grab. She also had him string beads, pick up little balls with tweezers, and react to noises. She suspected TJ had dyspraxia, which includes coordination difficulties, speech delay, learning difficulties, and sometimes persistent drooling.

At home, we noticed TJ's lack of response to us. He seemed not to notice Jack, even during his rages. TJ also began exhibiting some behaviors beyond the typical "terrible twos." He began using his hands more, and his tantrums often crossed over into the meltdown category. A temper tantrum is different from a meltdown, although the two terms are often used interchangeably. A temper tantrum is just what it sounds like: a child willfully acts out for attention or to get what he or she wants. There's an end goal. A meltdown can be caused by over or under stimulation, internal frustration, or anxiety. The person has little control once a meltdown begins.

TJ loves cars. He's very particular about the placement of his Hot Wheels. He lines them up in a big parade and becomes upset if one is kicked out of place in the line. TJ is a sensory seeker who responds to touch. He still requests I lay with him and rub his back at night. His memory is unbelievable. The facts he retains about space, cars, and states and capitals never ceases to amaze us.

We took TJ to Dr. Confidence in order to rule out a hearing problem. He passed his vision and hearing screenings without incident. Dr. Confidence agreed that TJ was speech delayed and probably had dyspraxia. It was Celeste who suggested we evaluate further.

Celeste was in a unique position to observe TJ in the waiting room when I brough Jack to social group. Just like at home, TJ would line up toys. When it came time to leave, TJ would struggle. Transitions were a huge obstacle for TJ. Often, I had to carry him past the (in my mind) judgmental looks in the waiting room and out to the car.

Being a special needs mom has given me a plethora of compassion. I've learned both as a special needs mom and a writer that there is always a backstory. I never assume a kid is "too old to be acting like that." I try never to assume, period.

"Have you thought about getting him evaluated?" Celeste asked one evening as I was carrying TJ out. "Autism can run in families."

Both Jack and TJ struggled with transitions. They both had some idiosyncrasies. While Jack didn't always know when to stop, TJ rarely engaged, especially verbally. While Jack avoided loud noises, strong smells, and crowds, TJ sought stimulation and was often the one making the loud noises, much to Jack's dismay. He would touch and sometimes even lick things. He chewed on sleeves and zippers. The biggest difference between the boys was their meltdowns. TJ's meltdowns could be long lasting, but his eyes didn't glaze over the way Jack's did. He could still be reached. When TJ melted down he was still TJ. He didn't go somewhere else.

I didn't want to wait like we had with Jack. This time, Luke was more receptive to an evaluation. The process was similar, but more focused on play. Neither of us were surprised when TJ was diagnosed with autism spectrum disorder.

The diagnosis meant TJ was qualified to attend a special education preschool. I was sad to leave Good Shepherd, but I knew TJ would have the invaluable benefit of a special education teacher, occupational therapist, and speech pathologist. We also set up ABA therapy. A therapist came into our home several days a week for two to three hours at a time to work with TJ. They even came with us on outings, teaching us to deal with transitions and elopement. The scariest part of going out and about with TJ was his tendency to suddenly take off, oblivious to danger. He wasn't running away as much as he was running toward something, but he lacked the insight and the verbal skills to communicate his intentions. The ABA therapists were paramount in helping us navigate these issues.

By the time TJ was diagnosed, we were fully immersed in the world of special needs. While every individual with autism is different, the differences between Jack and TJ, namely the meltdowns, made me question Jack's diagnosis. Also, with TJ some days were better than others, but his symptoms didn't disappear the way Jack's did.

Between the ages of seven and nine, Jack functioned typically for months at a time before he'd be stolen away again. Through all of the therapy one question remained. How could we shield Jack from a kidnapper we couldn't see? Did Jack have autism, and if not, what was really going on?

25

PANDAS

What if they do not believe me or listen to me?
—Exodus 4:1

February 2018–July 2018

My suspicions were confirmed when a follow-up psych eval failed to replicate Jack's autism diagnosis. Jack was diagnosed with generalized anxiety, persistent depressive disorder, and mild executive functioning difficulties.

"You mentioned you have depression," Lexi said to me after this diagnosis. "Is there a lot of talk about depression in your home?"

Her question again made me wonder if this was all my fault. While I didn't talk much about my depression, I didn't hide it either. When Jack asked why I took medicine every day I explained to him that sometimes my brain has difficulty producing enough of the chemicals I need to feel okay, but it was managed with medication and therapy. Jack didn't question it further.

We began keeping track of patterns. We eliminated food dyes. If Jack had a single lollipop, we'd see aggression. The biggest connection seemed to be illnesses or even allergies. When Jack contracted a virus or an allergen was particularly high, we could anticipate the kidnapper coming in about a week's time.

We tried to keep Jack as healthy as possible. We experimented with vitamin C, vitamin D, Omega-3s, even CBD oil. We took Jack to the chiropractor and sanitized our hands frequently to keep viruses at bay. Viruses allowed the kidnapper a portal into Jack's precious brain.

In February of 2018, Jack contracted the flu, determined by a nasal swab. Jack was prescribed Tamiflu. Hoping it would decrease the duration of the virus and maybe stop a flare, we picked it up from the pharmacy and gave Jack the first dose. He rested on the couch, and I continuously gave him water and ginger ale through a straw.

Jack was almost asleep that night when he sat bolt upright in bed. "Mom," he said in a groggy, disembodied voice, "can you tell them to stop laying the flooring? They're keeping me awake. It's so loud."

A chill ran through me in the otherwise cozy room. I followed Jack's gaze around the room as though I could see through his eyes. Was he dreaming? No, he hadn't even fallen asleep yet. I looked at Jack's eyes. They were piercing, gazing intently at something only he could see. The other possibility was terrifying to consider. *Was Jack hallucinating?*

Of course, I knew high fevers could cause hallucinations, but Jack's temperature was not significantly elevated. He'd been out of it all day; maybe the virus was affecting his brain.

"Lay down, Jack. No one's here. You're okay."

Jack looked at me in confusion, but he lay down and rolled over onto his side, his hands over his ears. I rubbed his back until he drifted off to sleep.

Jack spent the next day on the couch. Like Deja Vue, after we finished books that night Jack sat upright. This time he pushed his hands out in front of him repeatedly, like he was attempting to push something away.

"Mom?" Jack called in a loud voice as though I was in another room instead of right next to him, "Can you please help me get out of this computer?" He sounded more annoyed than scared. I couldn't say the same for myself.

I reached out and gently shook Jack's shoulder. "I'm right here, Jack. You're in bed. You're okay." I called for Luke to come in.

"Okay, but how do I get out of the computer?" He grunted in frustration while he tried to break free from the imaginary screen.

"Jack, I think you're dreaming," Luke said. "There's no computer. You're in bed."

"No, I'm not. I'm in a computer screen. How do I get out?"

I took Jack in my arms and rocked him like he was a baby again. His body stilled in my arms. Eventually, he looked up at me.

"Thanks for helping me get out. Will you lay with me until I fall asleep?"

I swallowed hard. "Of course, sweet boy." I grabbed the temporal thermometer and took his temperature. It was back to normal.

The next day, Luke and I talked about what had happened. "Is it the flu?" I wondered. "He's never hallucinated before."

"Could it be the Tamiflu?" Luke asked. "Let's skip it tonight and see how he sleeps."

I couldn't believe I hadn't thought of that. Both the doctor and the pharmacist assured me it was completely safe. The pamphlet that came with the medication didn't say a word about hallucinations.

I did what I should have done in the first place and conducted my own research. For the average person, it seems Tamiflu is safe and effective. However, I did read a few terrifying reports of young children hallucinating, including an instance in which a six-year-old attempted to jump from her second-story window. Of course, we couldn't be sure it was the Tamiflu, but we stopped it and Jack slept peacefully.

--- --- --- --- --- --- --- --- --- --- --- --- --- --- --- ---

Jack improved within a few days, but I remained on high alert. I'd been researching PANDAS. After our conversation, Charlotte had connected me with a PANDAS parent's group on Facebook. The more I researched, the more the pieces fit. I brought PANDAS up with Dr. Confidence, but he knew little about it. I brought my research to Luke.

"Hun, you wanted an answer. We had an evaluation. I think we need to trust what the professionals say."

Jack did so well for so long, I began second guessing myself. I wanted to believe we were "out of the woods" as they say in the medical community. It's a curious phrase, isn't it? Anyway, when Jack's evaluation at eight concluded that he was not in fact on the spectrum, I wondered again about PANDAS—that is, when I wasn't too busy blaming myself for "causing" Jack's depression. The self-blame distracted me from the real enemy. Talk about being lost in the woods.

When Jack got the flu, I considered it an opportunity for an experiment. Once Jack's symptoms subsided, I looked at the calendar. With a pen, I marked a day six days out. "Let's see," I said to Luke. "Let's just see if his behavior, if his *personality* changes right around here."

Luke shrugged the way he did when he meant to placate me. "Okay, hun, but I think you're reading into things. You don't always have to find reasons."

"Let's just see."

Exactly six days later, Jack was lying on the bench at the kitchen table screaming, his spelling sheets strewn on the floor around him in a crumpled mess.

"Jack, do your schoolwork," Luke said. "Sit up and do it!"

"This is last week's work. I don't have to do it!" He sat up long enough to fire a pencil across the table at Luke. Luke rounded the table and sat Jack up. He flopped like a ragdoll. "You're mean! I *hate* you!"

I watched the three words no parent wants to hear hit Luke like a physical blow. Luke let go of Jack and threw his hands up. "Fine." He retreated to the front room.

Jack flopped back on the bench with an animalistic roar. I looked at him. His eyes stared back at me, unseeing. I looked at the pen mark on the calendar. That was the moment I knew beyond a doubt. Spelling was the least of our problems. Jack had PANDAS.

I went into the front room where TJ was obliviously lining up cars. Luke was sitting on the worn couch with his head in his hands. My heart broke for all of us.

I sat next to Luke and put my hand on his back. "He didn't mean it. He loves you. The real Jack would never say that."

He looked up at me with tears in his eyes. "I don't know."

I swallowed, choosing my words carefully. "It's been exactly six days since the flu resolved. Every time he recovers from so much as a cold, he changes." Luke's expression was guarded, but I forged ahead. "He has PANDAS, Luke."

"He doesn't have PANDAS, Hope. You talked to the doctor about this. The counselors haven't even heard of it."

"Exactly! They don't know about it."

"And you do?"

"I've been researching. What about the articles I sent you? Don't they fit? We need to take him to see a specialist."

Luke shot to his feet as though I'd lit a fuse. He raked a hand through his hair. When he looked at me, his eyes were pained. "How many, Hope? How many specialists do you want to take him to? How much are we going to put him through? How many diagnoses do you need?"

"I just want the right one," I said, stung. "This isn't my fault, Luke."

"I never said it was. Of course, it's not your fault."

"If we don't find the right diagnosis, we can't find the right treatment. Answer me this—why was he diagnosed with autism at six but not at eight? Autism doesn't come and go. Why do his symptoms come and go?"

"I don't know." Luke shook his head. "I don't know, but the therapy with Lexi seems to be helping. A lot of times he goes to his room by himself to calm down. He's been doing so well. Maybe this is just a temporary setback." His eyes were pleading. He wanted so badly to believe that. I understood.

"It's a setback on the heels of a virus."

"But he's never even had a positive strep test."

"It could be a dormant infection. It doesn't even have to be strep. It all started with that virus he had right before he turned three. There's a PANDAS specialist in Hinsdale, but he's hard to get in to, and he doesn't take insurance."

"Let's wait, Hope."

"Wait? Wait for what? How much more childhood does he have to lose?"

"Exactly! Exactly, Hope. How much more of his childhood is he supposed to spend in doctors' offices and on therapists' couches? How much more testing is he supposed to go through? I just want him to have a normal, happy childhood like any other boy."

"That's what I want." My tone was measured. "You don't think that's what I want? That's what I'm fighting for, and lately"—I took a breath—"lately I feel like I'm fighting alone."

"Well, I'm sorry you feel that way, Hope, I really do. I know you want the best for him, and I respect your research. But I can't get on board with this. No more."

We went on like this. I can't stress enough how much strain special needs parenting puts on the strongest marriages. Luke and I slogged on through IEP meetings for TJ and ups and downs with Jack. While other parents carted their kids to little league games, soccer practice, and music lessons, we ran between therapy appointments. We moved like a car with three wheels; but we kept going.

I stayed up full nights researching. I learned that PANDAS was controversial. I watched a documentary entitled *My Kid Is Not Crazy*. I turned to the PANDAS parents group. It became my community, and I often found myself there while the rest of the house slept.

It was there that I learned I was far from the only parent dismissed by doctors, therapists, and even family. I even found stories of families with CPS in their lives. Ours was far from the only family divided. It was also where I learned of a 20/20 episode on PANDAS airing July 18, 2018. I saw another opportunity and asked Luke to watch the documentary with me. He agreed.

We set it to record and sat down to watch it once the kids were in bed. While difficult to watch, it was eye-opening seeing these children who'd changed overnight. Stories included a four-year-old placed in a psych ward and a girl who became terrified to swallow food. One father spoke candidly about the strain PANDAS put on his marriage, sharing that he hadn't believed his wife at first. Finally, a father likened it to an abduction. He said it was like someone coming in during the night and taking your child.

He looked at the camera and snapped his fingers. "Your kid is gone. Like, gone."

It was at that moment in the episode that Luke looked at me. I knew what people meant when they described seeing a lightbulb go off in someone's head. His face was dead white.

"This is it," my husband said to me. "Jack has PANDAS."

26

THE DIAGNOSIS PART 2

Let us hold unswervingly to the hope we profess,
for He who promised is faithful.

—Hebrews 10:23

October 31, 2018

Dr. K looked over Jack's writing samples, some neat and others nearly illegible depending on whether or not he was in a flare. He listened intently. Finally, he looked at me. "Before doing bloodwork or any diagnostics and after assessing Jack and talking to you, I can tell you with 80 percent certainty that your son has PANDAS."

There it was. The relief was palpable. Someone was finally listening. Someone—a doctor—believed me. Someone knew how to help. After six long years, we had an answer. The kidnapper had a name, and it was PANDAS.

PANDAS stands for pediatric autoimmune neuropsychiatric disorders associated with strep. According to the PANDAS network (pandasnetwork.org), PANDAS occurs when infection triggers a misdirected immune response and results in inflammation in a child's brain. In turn, the child quickly develops life-changing symptoms such as OCD, anxiety, tics, personality changes, and more. The hallmark trait of PANDAS is a sudden, acute, and debilitating onset of intense anxiety and mood lability accompanied by obsessive compulsive like issues and/or tics in association with a streptococcal-A infection that has occurred immediately prior to the symptoms (pandasnetwork.org).

The terms PANS (pediatric acute-onset neuropsychiatric syndrome) is sometimes used when strep cannot be identified as the trigger, but Dr. K prefers using the term PANDAS exclusively.

Dr. Susan Swedo pegged PANDAS in 1996 while studying Sydenham Chorea, a rare childhood disorder which can occur with rhematic fever. Both PANDAS and Sydenham Chorea affect the basil ganglia (pandasnetwork.org/medical-information). Dr. Swedo worked with a child who experienced tics and screaming rages following infection. According to Dr. Swedo, "PANDAS is distinguished from OCD and tic disorders, and eating disorders by the fact that there's an unusually abrupt onset. It literally comes on overnight" (from the documentary *My Kid Is Not Crazy*).

PANDAS, as Dr. K explained to me, is an autoimmune disease that, unlike other autoimmune diseases, attacks the brain. The body is met with an infection or a virus and a normal immune response is triggered. White blood cells begin attacking the intruder. When the illness resolves, the body fails to recognize its absence. The white blood cells enter the brain through the smell nerve and attack the basal ganglia, causing inflammation. I think we could see evidence of this inflammation in Jack's dilated pupils, which, according to Dr. K, is present in 83 percent of patients. Dr. K shares a link on his website (www.webpediatrics.com/pandas.html) detailing the signs and symptoms of PANDAS and the percentage of patients in which they occur.

OCD symptoms (intrusive thoughts, anxiety, phobias, unfounded fears, and repetitive physical and mental behaviors) are present in virtually all cases. Other symptoms include sleep disorders (84%), behavior regression such as separation anxiety and "baby talk" (98%), aggression (62%), hyperactivity and inattentiveness (71%), inability to concentrate (87%), hallucinations (9%), eating disorders (17%), deterioration in handwriting (72%), adventitious movements (31%), short-term memory loss (62%), urinary frequency (88%), and increased sensitivity to light, sounds, touch, and/or smell (39%). Also commonly reported are nonspecific gastrointestinal complaints. Most interesting and telling from this website was the sudden (sometimes overnight) onset of symptoms and the wax-and-wane pattern of the symptoms, namely following an infectious event. This was Jack.

I share all of this information with you not to bore or bombard you, but to inform you of what I myself didn't know—might never have known if not for my conversation with Charlotte. If one parent reads this book and thinks "this could be my child" then Jack's suffering, our suffering will not have been in vain. God kept his promise to me, and I will keep my promise to Him to share our story.

- -

"There is no definitive 'yes or no' bloodwork for PANDAS." Dr. K explained, "But there are diagnostic criteria. First, we do bloodwork. I will order a PANDAS panel to check strep titers, as well as to look for other markers, but the bloodwork alone will not confirm nor rule out diagnosis. We also start a fourteen-day course of antibiotics. During this time, I want you and your husband to conduct your own independent observations of Jack. Note any changes or improvements in symptoms and behavior. Email me at the end of the fourteen days."

I nodded, writing furiously in my notebook, wanting to absorb every word. I looked up. "What if we don't see a change with the antibiotics?"

Dr. K nodded knowingly. "Sometimes we don't. That doesn't mean he doesn't have PANDAS. If there's an insignificant response to antibiotics, we do a five-day steroid burst. If we notice a response with the steroids—improvement in behavior and functioning or cessation of symptoms, the diagnosis is 95 percent confirmed."

"What is the treatment?"

Dr K held up one finger. "First, get his tonsils and adenoids removed. Call Dr. Mahoney right away. She's right here in Hinsdale. Sometimes it takes a while to get into her. After that, we proceed with an IVIG procedure. I have greater success and lower rate of relapse if the tonsils and adenoids are removed prior to IVIG treatment. It's also most successful if conducted prior to the onset of puberty, but we can talk more about that at our next visit. Come back and see me after the surgery." Dr. K picked up an old-school prescription pad and scrawled out scripts for bloodwork, Augmentin, and prednisone.

Before I left, the angel in the white lab coat gave me the best news I've heard.

"Autism itself cannot be cured. This? This can be cured."

27

TREATMENT

*I performed my signs among them, and that
you may know that I am the Lord.*

—Exodus 10:2

November 2018–December 2018

We filled the antibiotics immediately. Four days in, we saw the real Jack shine through. He got up with his brother, helped him get dressed, and was very sweet. We saw more glimpses of Jack than we had in a long time, but they didn't last. He had a few meltdown and tic-free days, but his symptoms did not completely resolve during the fourteen-day trial.

Luke and I reported back to Dr. K, who was not surprised by the results and instructed us to fill the five-day course of prednisone, and then report back after an additional fourteen days.

Luke took Jack for his blook work. He was typically less reactive with Luke, so I stayed home with TJ. Luke and Jack reported that the blood work had been rough, to say the least. My poor Jack is terrified of needles. It took four adults to hold my child down so the nurse could draw his blood, plus Luke holding his hand and trying to console him. Nonetheless, we'd explained to Jack the importance of the blood test. He was scared, but he knew he had to do it.

"I just want to get better," he'd said when we told him about it. "I don't want to be like this anymore."

"We love you just the way you are, Jack. We're going to help you in any way we can."

Dr. K got back to us within the week. Jack's bloodwork was completely normal, which he told us is not uncommon in PANDAS. Per his instruction, we proceeded with the steroid burst. The results were remarkable.

"I feel better," Jack reported with a smile on day two.

"That's great!" I said. "Better how?"

"Um, I don't know. Happier. More peaceful."

"That's great, sweetie." I gave him a giant hug.

By day two on the steroid, Jack's throat clearing, tongue clicking, and baby-talk had disappeared, along with his meltdowns. Jack was vibrant, even bubbly for a solid two weeks. I happily reported the news to Dr. K. At the time, I was still confused on the term "PANS" and also reflected on the fact that Jack had never had a positive strep culture. I wished I'd known to push for a strep culture when he got the mysterious virus right before his third birthday.

"Response to steroid burst makes the diagnosis of PANDAS 90 to 95 percent certain despite negative bloodwork," Dr. K told me in a follow-up email. "Just because you cannot recall strep infections and his bloodwork was negative does NOT mean he did not have strep previously. I personally hate "PANS" term since it doesn't mean anything."

Jack's improvements from the steroid burst didn't maintain, which of course we expected. The next step was a consultation with an ear, nose, and throat doctor Dr. K had recommended. December 11, 2018, the day after TJ's sixth birthday found us in the office of Dr. Mahoney. I read the boys books in the waiting room. After about twenty minutes we were called back.

"Jack was diagnosed with PANDAS," I told the young Latina nurse taking Jack's vitals. I braced myself for the raised eyebrows and the skepticism, but the kind man merely nodded.

"Oh, yeah, okay. Dr. Mahoney gets a lot of PANDAS patients. Do you see Dr. Kovacevic?"

"Yes. He referred us here."

The man nodded. "Dr. Mahoney will be in shortly."

Dr. Mahoney was kind. She cared; I could tell as soon as she entered the gray and pink exam room with her blond wavy hair and open smile.

"I'm so sorry for the wait." A slight sheen of sweat shined on her forehead.

I smiled. "No, problem. TJ, don't touch that."

"TJ. Hi, TJ. You're being very patient. How old are you?"

TJ stared at her.

"TJ," I prompted, "how old are you?"

"Six. My birthday was yesterday."

"Wow, six! Happy birthday, young man. Tell you what? Since your birthday was yesterday and you're waiting so patiently, you can pick two prizes from my toybox once I'm done talking to your mom and examining your brother. Sound good?"

"Yeah."

"Say thank you, TJ."

"Thank you."

"And you must be Jack." She turned her attention to Jack sitting on the narrow rubber table with a paper runner. "I'm Dr. Mahoney. It's nice to meet you." She held out her hand.

"Nice to meet you." Jack took her proffered hand and offered her a guarded smile. I liked her right away, and I think Jack did too.

Jack gagged when she put a tongue depressor in his mouth. She winced. "Sorry, hunny. So Dr. K sent you? He's the absolute best."

"Yes, he was very impressive. He spoke highly of you as well. He diagnosed Jack with PANDAS. I was told by so many professionals that PANDAS wasn't a thing or that Jack didn't have it. Some hadn't even heard of it."

She shook her head and frowned. "Isn't that something? Dr. Kovacevic is an amazing doctor. He's spoken about PANDAS all over the globe. He's an advocate. He really loves his kids."

"Yes, he seems to."

She looked in Jack's throat and nose with a light. "You know, his tonsils are slightly enlarged, but they don't look too bad. He has a lot of mucous in his nose."

"He has trouble blowing it. We see a chiropractor to help with that and overall immunity."

She nodded. "Good. Do you get sore throats, Jack?"

"Sometimes. Not really."

"We had him allergy tested at our previous ENT, but nothing specific turned up. He coughs and sneezes a lot, especially when he first wakes up."

"What did your previous ENT say about his tonsils and adenoids?"

"He said they were fine, and they didn't need to come out, but Dr. K thinks they do. What do you think?"

"Well, of course, it's always your choice. I've been working with Dr. Kovacevic for many years. He's taught me many things, namely, IVIG—if you choose to do it—has a higher success rate if the tonsils and adenoids come out first. Removal of tonsils and adenoids is indicated in PANDAS treatment. Also, just because the tonsils don't look bad doesn't mean they aren't potentially loaded with bacteria and infection. A lot of that I can't see just by looking in his throat. If we proceed with the surgery, I'll send the tissue to the lab for testing." Dr. Mahoney snapped her gloves off and rolled her stool over to the garbage can under the sink. "As I said, it's always your choice, and you don't have to decide today. Now, what questions do you have for me?"

"What's the recovery like?" I hated putting Jack through pain, no matter how necessary.

"Full recovery usually takes ten to fourteen days. He can return to school after a week. He can eat soft foods—whatever he can tolerate. We alternate Tylenol and Motrin for pain. The most important thing is to keep the throat wet and keep him hydrated. Some kids don't want to drink afterward, but it's crucial to push fluids. Do you have any questions for me, Jack?"

"I don't want to get needles."

Dr. Mahoney smiled knowingly. "Don't worry, you won't feel the IV. We put a little mask on you that makes you go right to sleep.

We put the IV in once you're already asleep. You won't know it's happening. You won't feel the surgery itself at all."

"What if I wake up during the surgery?"

"Oh, you won't, hunny. We have a doctor called an anesthesiologist in the operating room to monitor you and make sure you stay asleep. Mom and Dad can stay with you right up until you go back. Then you go right to sleep."

He nodded solemnly. "Okay."

"Here's a pamphlet of information. Go home, read it, and talk it over. There's no rush."

"If we decide to schedule, do we just call the office?"

"Yep. Call the front desk and they'll take care of you. It was nice to meet you guys. Pick out two toys each from the prize bin in the hallway."

TJ picked out a Hot Wheels car and a bouncy ball. Jack picked stickers and a mini monster truck. "Here you go, TJ. You can have this. I know how much you love monster trucks."

I swallowed a lump in my throat. "That was really thoughtful, Jack. TJ, what do you say to your brother?"

"Thank you, Jack."

Once we returned to the car Jack began to cry softly. "I don't want to get the surgery."

"I know, sweetie. But out of your whole life, two weeks of recovery is worth it. It's worth it if it's a step toward you feeling better, right?"

Jack sniffled. "I guess."

"If I could do it for you, I would. So would Dad."

"I know."

"Tell you what? We're heading to San Diego in a little over a week. Let's look forward to a trip and spending Christmas with our family. We can talk about the surgery after our trip and the holidays, okay?"

"Okay."

The boys had been looking forward to the trip to my brother and sister-in-law's house for months. I didn't want Jack's trip to be tainted by thoughts of surgery. I was determined to put this aside and fill Jack with excitement and joy.

I wasn't sure I could do the same for myself. I had to talk to Luke, but I didn't need time to think about it; I already knew. God had led us to Dr. K, and we had to trust him.

Jack had to have the surgery.

28

SURGERY

Trust in the Lord with all your heart and lean not on
your own understanding.; in all your ways submit to
Him, and He will make your path's straight.

—Proverbs 3:5–6

April 15, 2019–May 6, 2019

Jack, Luke, and I waited in a surprisingly spacious hospital room
watching the sun come up. Luke's mom Lorraine was at our house
to get TJ up and off to school. I was grateful we could place our sole
focus on Jack, and grateful Luke was there.

I helped our brave boy into a blue and white gown. "I love your
hat, sir," I said in a silly voice while I fixed the blue mesh over Jack's
hair.

"Looking good, bud," Luke added from his spot in the chair
against the wall. He took a sip of tepid coffee and winced. Dark circles under his eyes betrayed his stress. He offered me a pained smile.

I fought off tears before turning back to Jack. "Are you cold,
sweetie? Do you want to get under the blanket?"

"No, thanks. When are they coming in?"

"Pretty soon. The nurse will give you some medicine to make
you feel calm and a little sleepy."

"Will it taste bad?" His beautiful eyes stared into mine, trusting me.

"I don't think so. I think they said it's cherry. Just swallow it down quickly." I gave Jack a tight squeeze. "I'm so proud of you. You're so brave." I turned away from my hospital gown—clad little boy under the guise of taking a sip of my own coffee, abandoned on the air conditioner. *If only.* If only I could have the surgery instead. My heart went out to parents of injured or chronically ill children. I felt for parents who had to watch helplessly, able to offer only a modicum of comfort while their children went through painful but necessary procedures. I ached for all families who had to spend more time in hospitals and doctors' offices than at home.

Luke set his coffee on the scratched linoleum floor and came over. He squeezed my shoulder and then Jack's. "Everything will be okay."

I knew this was hurting Luke. Like many men, Luke is a fixer. He's a protector. He couldn't fix this, and he couldn't protect Jack—not from the pain of surgery and not from the kidnapper. Yet this was the next step toward eradicating the kidnapper. God, through Dr. K, could fix this. *This can be cured.*

"Knock, knock." A nurse with long brown hair wearing cheery pink and blue scrubs with little white dogs on them entered. She carried a little plastic cup half filled with cherry-red liquid. "I have some medicine here. It's cherry."

Jack swallowed the medicine. They had him get into bed. We walked beside him as he was wheeled to the elevator. We wound up in a curtained off room while we waited. I tried to distract Jack with funny videos on my phone.

"Hello, it's nice to see you again." Dr. Mahoney came in and shook my hand. She turned to Luke and held out her hand. "I'm Dr. Mahoney."

"Luke."

"It's nice to meet you. Do you have any questions for me?"

"No, I think my wife explained everything." He rubbed my back.

"Hi, Jack. How are you doing?"

"Okay. Scared. Will it hurt?"

"You won't feel the surgery at all. You'll be totally asleep. You'll have a sore throat afterward, but we'll give you medicine to help with that. Make sure to drink a lot to keep your throat moist. You can also have popsicles, slushies, and ice cream."

Soon it was time. We held Jack's hands all the way to the operating room doors. "We'll be right here when you wake up," I told Jack, swallowing my own apprehension.

"Love you, bud. We'll be waiting." Luke let go of Jack's hand and took mine.

"Bye, Mom. Bye, Dad." Jack waved sleepily as he was wheeled through the doors.

I wiped my eyes when the doors closed, hiding Jack away from us. I wanted to run after them—to burst through the doors, grab Jack, and run.

Luke put his arm around my shoulders and squeezed. "He'll be okay."

I leaned into him, comforted as always by his proximity and touch. Hand in hand, we walked to the surgical waiting room. While we waited, I retrieved my notebook from my bag and tried to write, but it was impossible to get more than a few sentences down. I could do little more than watch the clock and fixate on the TV screen that told families where their loved ones were in the surgical process.

"He's still in the operating room," I told Luke. "Do you think everything's okay?"

He placed a stilling hand on my bouncing leg. "I do. The doctor said it would be over an hour." He checked his watch. "It's only been twenty minutes."

"Only twenty minutes?" I sighed. "Are we wrong for putting him through this?"

Luke stopped typing on his laptop and fixed his piercing blue eyes on me. "No. You were right all along, Hope. You knew what he needed. Don't second-guess yourself now."

I nodded. "I know. I know it's necessary. I believe 100 percent that God led us to Dr. K, and we need to follow what he said. I just wish he didn't have to go through it. I'm worried he'll be in a lot of pain afterward."

"We'll help him through it."

I paused. "I feel like we'll need to do the IVIG too. It sounds extreme and I'd like to avoid it, but I don't want the surgery to be for nothing."

"Let's take one thing at a time, sweetie. Dr. K wants to see Jack four weeks after surgery, right? Let's focus on his recovery for now."

"No, you're right." I watched the screen until Jack moved to the recovery room.

Finally, Dr. Mahoney came in. Luke and I got to our feet. "He did great," she said quickly. "He's not quite awake yet, but you guys can come back and be with him."

We hastily packed up our stuff and followed Dr. Mahoney back to the curtained area. Jack was lying under a white blanket. An IV line ran from under the blanket to a bag. Jack's eyes were closed. His face was crunched up. Tears streaked from his closed lids.

Luke gently rubbed Jack's arm. "Hey, bud."

I smoothed Jack's hair back and rubbed his forehead. "Hi, sweetie. Dad and I are here. You're okay."

Jack opened his mouth. His lips were dry. "Mommy, ow."

"I know, sweetie. I know."

"Mom, you can lay with him," Dr Mahoney said, as though reading my thoughts. She lowered the bedrail on one side. I scooted onto the narrow bed and took Jack in my arms, being careful not to bump the IV. Jack whimpered.

"Can we do anything to make him more comfortable?" I asked.

Dr. Mahoney rubbed the crease in Jack's forehead. "It's okay, hunny. I'll get him something for the pain, okay?"

"Thank you," I said.

"Thank you, Doctor," Luke echoed.

She returned promptly and put medicine into Jack's IV line. Instantly, he relaxed. We were wheeled back to the room with Luke following along. Jack woke up enough for me to feed him a red popsicle before dropping back to sleep. I let him sleep as much as possible but woke him frequently to spoon ice chips into his mouth and coax him to take sips of water.

Hours went by. Luke left to get TJ from school. He'd then make the thirty-minute drive back to pick us up, allowing Jack more time to rest before the drive home. I didn't move from Jack's bed. He'd get through this. I'd do everything in my power to comfort him and limit the pain. We'd get Jack through this. We'd pay the ransom and get Jack back for good. I replayed Dr. K's words in my head like a mantra.

"This can be cured."

29

RECOVERY

I consider that our present sufferings are not worth
comparing with the glory that will be revealed in us.
—Romans 8:18

April 2019–May 2019

"I can't stand the pain," Jack moaned, thrashing in his bed.

He'd awakened before the three-hour mark. It was too soon to give him more medicine. We were keeping Jack on a tight medication schedule, waking him every three hours to alternate Motrin and Tylenol in an effort to stay ahead of the pain. It wasn't working.

"Here, sweetie, let's take some sips of water." I helped him lift his head and brought the cup to his lips. He shook his head. "I know it hurts, but you have to drink. We don't want your throat to get dry. Let's try some ice first. I'll be right back."

I dashed downstairs and filled a cup with crushed ice, grateful for our ice maker. Grabbing a spoon, I rushed back to Jack's room. I spooned ice into his mouth and snuck in sips of water until it was time for his next dose of medicine. We were both able to get back to a fitful sleep until he woke two hours later and the whole cycle started over.

It's excruciating to witness your child in pain; it's a helpless feeling. Maybe my expectations were too high for night four after surgery, but the medicine, ice, and hydration weren't enough to give

Jack any relief. He wasn't eating. He wasn't sleeping. We were doing ice chips and pushing fluids nonstop. None of it was enough.

The discharge instructions listed reasons to contact the on-call number. One of those reasons was severe pain not controlled by medication. I left a message detailing the situation and requesting a call back. When an on-call doctor finally returned my call, he was the opposite of kind Dr. Mahoney.

"If he's getting enough fluids, there's not much we can do. If he won't drink or you feel he's dehydrated, take him to the ER for fluids," he told me.

"He's drinking, and I'm giving him ice chips and medication around the clock," I said.

"Alternate Tylenol and Motrin every three to four hours around the clock."

Didn't I just tell him that's what we're doing? "Yes, we are. It's not making a dent in the pain. He's been up every two hours screaming that his throat and ears hurt."

"Ear pain is normal after surgery. It's all normal. I know it's a lot to keep up with, but—"

"It's not about that." I was exasperated by this point. "I'm fine getting up with him. I anticipated pain after surgery, of course, but our discharge instructions said to call if he had pain not relieved by medication."

"You have to do it every three to four hours, even through the night."

Was this guy paying any attention to me? Was I interrupting his show or something?

"I am. We haven't missed a single dose."

"We don't give narcotics anymore."

I imagined him nodding while stroking a long-haired white cat. "I understand that. But is it normal for him to be in severe pain not relieved at all by medication?"

"Pain after surgery is normal, even severe pain. Keep giving the pain medicine every three to four hours and keep him hydrated."

I hung up feeling dismissed. Yet I'm not sure what I'd expected the doctor to offer. I don't know much about the short-term use of pain medication in children, but I can say with confidence that pain—both postsurgical and chronic—is undertreated in this country. Ask many doctors, and they'll disagree with this statement. In my nonmedical opinion and based on my own experience, allowing people to suffer with undertreated pain—"normal" or not—is unnecessarily cruel.

It wasn't the first time I'd been disregarded by someone in the medical profession, and it wouldn't be the last, but I'd learned not to waste my time. I'd learned to move on. Some people—even in the listening profession—are incapable of listening.

I don't want to go too far down the rabbit hole here, but I do want to say that many doctors, including my own, are fierce advocates for their patients. Unfortunately, though, others are simply not listening. If you're a doctor and you happen to be reading this, I don't care how many letters you have after your name, listen to your patients. Acknowledge their pain. They are the experts on their own bodies. Parents are the first experts on their children. Please listen. Lives and livelihoods depend on it.

*****

Easter Sunday fell six days after Jack's surgery. His sleepless nights continued. Luke and I took shifts getting up with Jack throughout the night. Easter is Jack's favorite holiday, but when the day came, he remained in bed, in too much pain and too exhausted to hunt for eggs. I brought him his Easter basket, but he couldn't muster up any interest.

Bleary-eyed and aching for Jack, I put on a brave face for TJ as I read him the clues for our scavenger hunt. Luke followed us, taking a video on his phone. Luke took TJ to my aunt and uncle's house for dinner and another egg hunt. It was another tradition Jack thoroughly enjoyed.

I set Jack up in our bed so he could watch TV. I lay next to him, offering him company, ice chips, and water. Both of us dozed off periodically while watching one of our favorite shows, *Tiny House Hunters*. A regular diet was allowed, but Jack had little interest in eating. He was still only tolerating extremely soft foods. He lost ten pounds. I'd hoped by Easter Jack would be further along in his recovery.

I'll never know for sure, but I wonder if PANDAS itself made Jack's recovery from the surgery more daunting. Other parents I knew whose children had gone through extraction of tonsils and adenoids had reported more manageable pain and faster recover. It's impossible to say as everyone recovers differently. With Jack, we saw a drastic change on day ten.

On April 24, nine days after surgery, Jack had a flare. Nothing in particular set him off (that we could tell). He screamed and cried. He ran through the house, throwing whatever he could get his hands on. He lunged at TJ and hit and pushed me. That night an exhausted Jack slept through the night for the first time since surgery. The next day—day ten—he woke up, and we knew the kidnapper had left.

Jack came downstairs and requested a waffle. He reported that his throat hurt but not as much, and his ears felt better. I'd expected a much more gradual recovery, but I was overjoyed to see Jack up and about with the color in his cheeks restored. More remarkable was his mood and behavior. He helped TJ get ready for school. He cooperated on his own schoolwork and focused on making his writing neat.

On May 5, Jack had another successful day of homeschooling. He asked if we could walk to pick up TJ from his elementary school a little over half a mile away. I would try to walk to pick up if it was mild enough, but Jack typically fought it. The walks—when they were possible at all—consisted of stomping, complaining, glaring, and dragging his feet. By the time we arrived at school, Jack would be furious, refusing to talk to TJ or me.

On May 5, Jack walked beside me, his disposition as sunny as the spring day. Jack had been spending a lot of time holed up in his room. We grew weary of the constant battle over computer time. On May 6, he told me he'd had enough and wanted to get some fresh air. He jumped on the trampoline and laughed with his brother.

I couldn't stop hugging Jack. My curious, helpful, sweet, sensitive boy was back, but I didn't know for how long.

30

⤬

IVIG

But I will keep hoping for your help; I will praise you more
and more. I will tell everyone about your righteousness.
—Psalm 71:14

We received Jack's toxicology report back at our follow-up with Dr.
Mahoney. Despite the fact that our previous ENT had told us Jack's
tonsils didn't need to come out and even though he'd never had a
positive strep test, the report showed that his tonsils were loaded
with strep. The results showed heavy growth of Streptococcus pneumonia, Streptococcus vividans group/two morphological types,
and Staphylococcus aureus. There was also moderate growth of
Haemophilus Influenza as well as micrococcus species and several
other bacteria. Dr. Mahoney explained that these infections had been
lying dormant in Jack's tonsils. For us, this confirmed that the surgery had been the right course of action.

Jack's allergies did not seem to change much, but his personality
and behavior did. Luke and I couldn't get over the improvements in
Jack. Previously withdrawn and spending a lot of time in his room,
Jack was coming downstairs in the morning ready to take on the
day. He got dressed and ready with little to no prompting and even
encouraged TJ to get ready. Jack was interacting positively with me.
He was asking to play Mrs. Antbottom, a game I'd invented when
Jack was in kindergarten. I played a teacher with a high-pitched voice

who took her class on field trips to "Mr. Jack's" block buildings. Jack was so engaged, and I savored every moment with the real Jack.

Another positive change I noted was Jack's willingness to do his schoolwork. He took his time on his writing and his penmanship improved. Several weeks went by without a rage or a meltdown. Jack remained in good spirits.

"The surgery seems to have really made a difference," Luke commented one night over dinner.

"Yeah," I agreed, picking up a piece of crusty bread. "The change is remarkable. I'm really glad all of that dormant strep and other bacteria is out of his body. It's amazing how much that was impacting his behavior. It makes you wonder how many people are living with autism, OCD, mood disorders, even schizophrenia, and the root cause is autoimmune. I mean, obviously mental illness exists in its own right; but some percentage of people are actually dealing with PANDAS, or something related. If we didn't know, imagine how many other parents don't."

Luke and I were on a much-needed date at a French restaurant near my mom's house. We were able to leave the kids with her while we had a quiet dinner. It was a perfect early summer night. We sat on the patio under a string of silver lights. I was buoyed by our success with Jack, and for the millionth time grateful to Charlotte, Dr. K, and God for making us aware of PANDAS and offering us the shiny irreplaceable gift of hope.

Luke took a sip of his Malbec. "Jack has been his usual jovial self. Even his writing's been better. It looks like we won't have to put him through the IVIG."

I paused, my champagne glass halfway to my mouth. I didn't want to put Jack through the IVIG either, of course. But I'd been praying about it and the still small voice of God within my heart was telling me it wasn't over yet. "I don't know, Luke. We're only a few weeks out from the surgery. Just because Jack hasn't had a flare since then doesn't mean he won't."

Luke frowned. "Can we just be patient?"

"I'm being patient. Believe me, I'm thrilled with his progress. When he's himself, I don't take one single moment with him for granted."

Luke's voice softened. "I know that, sweetie. IVIG seems extreme to me."

"It does. I don't want it to be traumatic for him. But mostly, I don't want to look back years later and say we should've done it. On that documentary we watched—*My Kid Is Not Crazy*—the one Dr. K was on, there was a family that said if they'd done IVIG their son would have a normal life. Instead, he's in a group home. I don't want that to be us. I don't want that to be Jack."

Luke set his glass down. "We can't see the future, Hope."

"We kind of can though, in this case. Dr. K says the highest success with the lowest rate of relapse occurs with IVIG following the removal of the tonsils and adenoids." I paused, taking a sip of my champagne. "I know it sounds strange to you, but I truly feel that God told me to trust Dr. K, and that the journey isn't over yet."

"I believe in God, Hope."

"I know, but do you ask for guidance? If you ask Him to help you hear His voice, He will. He led us to Dr. K, and I truly believe we have to follow his treatment protocol."

"Okay, okay. Can we talk about something else?"

I should've left it alone for the moment and enjoyed our dinner. Except, I couldn't. My life was the kids and getting them what they needed. I'd become consumed with getting Jack back—with vanquishing the kidnapper forever. I'd do anything to spare Jack from living with the abductor waiting in the shadows for the rest of his life.

"Hun, it's just that Dr. K told me the IVIG is most successful when done prior to puberty. Jack's nine. We don't have much time."

"I know how old he is. I just—can't we just enjoy dinner? This is our first date in weeks. We rarely get to talk. Can't we enjoy our time together?"

"Exactly, we rarely get to talk. We can't talk about this in front of the kids. What's more important?"

"Hope, we're not going to make this decision tonight. I need a chance to decompress after the work week, okay?"

Luke was right. We both needed time without the kids—time that wasn't all about the kids. But I pressed on. Like I said, I was consumed. "I'll fight for it if I have to."

"You don't have to fight me, Hope. I'm on your side. Let's see how he does, okay?"

I nodded. "Fair enough. I'm sorry, it's just so important. Will you come with us to our follow-up with Dr. K so you have a chance to ask him questions and bring up concerns? That way it won't be me relaying information second-hand. I think you'll be impressed with him."

"I'll check my work schedule. It should be doable."

"I really think it's important. Tell your boss you have an appointment with your son's doctor. I'm sure he'll understand."

"It's not about him not understanding. I have deadlines."

We have deadlines with Jack too, I thought bitterly. *Life-altering deadlines.*

Luke reached across the small table and grasped my hand. "I'm sure I can work it out. I want to be there. You're not in this alone, okay?"

I swallowed hard and squeezed his hand. "Okay."

*****

Luke and I dropped TJ off at my mom's house and made the thirty-minute drive to Dr. K's office. I tapped my pen on my notebook and fiddled with the radio while Luke drove.

"I don't want to see Dr. K again," Jack grumbled from the back seat.

"I know, Bean, but we're just going to talk to him and let him know how're you're doing," I assured him.

"Will he give me a shot?"

"Nope. No shots."

"But I don't want to get that needle thing done."

I glanced at Luke.

"We don't want you to have to get it done either, bud," he said. "We're not going to do anything today except talk to the doctor, okay?"

"Okay."

We pulled up to the red-brick building, and I led the way to Dr. K's office.

"Hello, again." The receptionist smiled. I paid, and she led us right in.

"Hello, Mary Lou." Dr. K tapped Jack on the head with a file folder.

Jack smirked and rolled his eyes.

Dr. K held out his hand to Luke. "I'm Dr. K. It's nice to meet you."

"Luke. Nice to meet you, Doctor."

Dr. K patted the white paper covered table. "Hop up," he said to Jack.

Jack looked at Dr. K suspiciously but climbed onto the table.

Dr. K looked in Jack's nose and mouth. "Did you have a follow-up with Dr. Mahoney?"

"Yes," I said. "We brought a copy of the toxicology report for you. Jack's tonsils were loaded with strep."

Dr. K nodded. "I'm not surprised." He took the paper from me. "A positive rapid strep test is not necessary for the diagnosis of PANDAS. How have things been since the surgery?"

"Well, the recovery was rough," I said. "But by day ten he turned the corner. I'd say he's been really good since then. School is going well. He hasn't had any meltdowns or rages."

"Good. That shows us how much the bacteria was affecting him." He turned back to Jack. "How are you feeling since the surgery, Jack?"

Jack shrugged. "Good. Better."

Dr. K swiveled on his stool and faced Luke and me. "I'm very encouraged by the results. The next step is the IVIG. Like I said, my success rate with IVIG after tonsils and adenoid removal is quite high."

"Doctor," Luke said, "is the IVIG necessary, given the results we've seen since surgery?"

"It's a good question. He's doing well now, but he *will* have another flare. Take your time to think about it and call when you're ready."

I looked from Luke to Dr. K. "Don't we need to do it before puberty?"

"Ideally, yes. He's nine, so you have a little time. How about you enjoy the summer, and we touch base in the fall? That's when I expect another flare, once cold and flu season arrives." Dr. K turned to Luke. "What are your concerns with the IVIG?"

He winced. "It seems extreme to me. What are the risks? How does it work?"

"You don't need to worry. The risks are low. There's a very small risk of infection. That's it."

"What about the side effects?"

"Some kids have none. A percentage will get headache, some nausea, possible fatigue, and low-grade fever the first three days following the IVIG. The recovery is nothing compared to the tonsils and adenoids surgery."

"How does it work?" I asked. I'd been researching IVIG, but I trusted Dr. K. I wanted to hear his explanation. I also wanted Luke to hear it.

"Jack will receive donor immunoglobulin. The infusion is comprised of thousands of donors. This will essentially rebuild his immune system."

"Will it hurt?" Jack asked, wide-eyed.

"There is an IV," Dr. K responded honestly. "The nurse will numb your hand or arm first. You'll feel a little pinch. Once it's in, you'll be comfortable in a bed or you can sit up and play video games. Once the IV is in we leave it in until we're done. It doesn't hurt once it's in. That's the only part of this that hurts at all. He turned back to us. "It's done at the Oakbrook Surgical Center. You'll go in on a Thursday morning, early. They'll give him a double dose of Benadryl, then he'll get numbed and we'll start the IV. The nurse will check on him every fifteen minutes or so. Now, very important that he drinks plenty of water throughout the infusion and after. That helps prevent the bad headache. About two thirty, you'll go home. We leave the IV in so they don't have to stick you again. Six thirty, Friday morning you return to the surgical center. They give him more Benadryl and start the infusion. Two thirty, you go home and then he's done."

177

"Does he have to isolate after?"

Dr. K shook his head. "He can return to school Monday. Make sure he drinks—preferably alkaline water. Other than that, he can do whatever he wants. I've had kids play soccer the next day."

"Wow." I glanced at Luke. He had that lightbulb look again.

"Thank you, Doctor," Luke said. "I feel better about it now, but I'd still like to wait and see how Jack does."

Dr. K nodded. "Of course. Take your time and enjoy your summer. I'll see you in the fall."

31

RANSOM

The Lord will fight for you; you need only be still.

—Exodus 14:14

September 2019

As Dr. K predicted, summer was uneventful. When the flare came in the fall, I don't think any of us were surprised. The IVIG procedure was scheduled for September 26 and 27. We had Lorraine lined up to come in the mornings until TJ got picked up from school by a neighbor. The only remaining step was to call the insurance company.

Dr. K's office had sent a request for coverage, but I hadn't heard back. With the procedure only weeks away, I did what my ADHD brain tries to avoid; I got on the phone. I sat at the kitchen table drumming my pen on my notebook while I waited through one automated message after another. Finally, I got through to an actual human.

"Hello, thank you for calling Insurance Company. This is Jodi. Can you verify your name and date of birth?"

I gave her the information and heard computer keys clacking.

"Yes, Jack Shepherd, birthdate 6/1/09, correct?"

"Yes."

"Okay, I'm showing here that coverage was denied."

I felt the blood drain from my face. "Why is that?"

`"Let me go ahead and check that for you." More clacking. "Okay, it says here that the procedure is not medically necessary," she said brightly.

I shot up from my seat and began to pace. Beads of perspiration broke at my temples.

"Can I help you with anything else?"

"I'm sorry, how was it determined that it's not medically necessary?" I choked out my words around the lump in my throat.

"I don't have that information," she said in the same bright voice, "but it looks like the decision has been made. Is there anything else I can help you with today?"

"I'm sorry," I said again, "but if his doctor, his *specialist* who has been treating him for a year determined that it's medically necessary, how can you as an insurance company say it's not?"

"I don't have that information."

"My child has been sick, suffering with this for six years. I'm not just going to accept that this procedure he needs is not covered."

"I'm so sorry, ma'am."

I took a deep breath. "I know it's not your fault. I'm not meaning to blame you."

"Oh no, that's okay."

"But," I continued as though she hadn't spoken, "we will take this further if we need to. We won't accept that it's not medically necessary. Is there a manager or someone I could talk to?"

"Yes. Please hold, and I'll transfer you."

"Thank you."

By this point, I was shaking. The phrase "not medically necessary" flashed in my brain in bold red letters. How dare they? How did these people sleep at night? My mind raced ahead. I wouldn't let this go. We'd appeal, but we were short on time. We'd pay if we had to; we'd find a way. No ransom was too high.

I'd practically worn a hole in the floor by the time the alleged manager came on the line. "Hello, Mrs. Shepherd?"

"Yes." I clenched my jaw.

"Hello, I'm Sarah. What can I help you with today?"

"I was told that an IVIG procedure for my son, Jack is not covered."

"Yes, I see that right here. Without a medical diagnosis, we deem this procedure not medically necessary."

"He's diagnosed with PANDAS."

"Yes, I see that diagnosis here. Unfortunately, that diagnosis is not eligible for coverage. We cover IVIG for autoimmune diseases and some other—"

"PANDAS is an autoimmune disease."

"Hmm, well, it's not listed here as such. Now, is there anything else I can—"

"Are you a doctor?" I was not about to be dismissed. "Because Dr. Kovacevic, who is a PANDAS specialist, does this procedure all the time, and he deemed it medically necessary for my son."

"No, ma'am, I'm personally not a doctor." Her tone had become frosty. I didn't care. "Our doctor on staff reviewed your son's case and denied it based on medical necessity."

"Your doctor has never seen nor treated my son. He's been dealing with this illness for six years."

We went back and forth on the appeal process. "Ma'am, if you don't want to appeal your only other option is to give your doctor's office a call back. You're going to want to ask your son's doctor to call our doctor and do what's called a peer-to-peer consult. Would you like the number for your doctor to call?"

"Yes, please."

She gave me an eight hundred number for Dr. K to call. "Then your doctor can discuss the case with our doctor, and our doctor will determine if the treatment is medically necessary for you son. Now, would you like me to give you the out-of-pocket cost, just in case?"

"Yes."

"Hold one moment please." Elevator music played in my ear until she returned. "It's sixty-five grams of immunoglobulin. That's $10,156.50 for the medication. Along with the procedure, that's $11,956.50."

Almost $12,000. Of course, if it came to that we'd pay. We'd do whatever we needed to do, no matter how high the ransom. Still, as far as I knew Illinois was the only state that required private insurance companies to cover IVIG for the treatment of PANDAS. I wasn't giving up without a fight.

My mind returned to the unnecessary controversy surrounding PANDAS. First, parents had to wade through the quicksand of misdiagnosis. Then, even with an accurate diagnosis, they were left to deal with astronomical medical costs. *Not medically necessary.* PANDAS is a medical diagnosis, plain and simple. Medical treatment for it is not a luxury but an absolute necessity for a life-altering, childhood-robbing MEDICAL diagnosis.

I headed upstairs to Jack's room, sat at his desk, opened my notebook, and called Dr. K's office.

"You guys are in Illinois," the kind receptionist said after I'd explained the insurance situation and she'd accessed our records.

"Yes," I said, unsure if it was a question or a statement. I knew many of Dr. K's patients came from out of state. PANDAS specialists were about as easy to find as unicorns.

"If you live in Illinois, the insurance company is required to cover IVIG for PANDAS treatment."

"That's what I thought. Shouldn't the insurance company know that?"

"Oh, they do," she said in a way that made me think she wasn't new to dealing with greedy insurance providers. "They know. They're counting on you not knowing. I'd call them again. In the meantime, I'll give the message to Dr. Kovacevic and he'll call their doctor. Please keep on them."

"I will, thank you." I gave her the number for Dr. K to call and hung up. I immediately grabbed my computer.

A fire had ignited within me. I knew my rights—Jack's rights. I wasn't about to allow an insurance company to skirt their responsibility. *Not medically necessary.* We'll see.

House Bill 2721, also known as "Charlie's Law" was passed into law on June 18, 2017, in the state of Illinois. The bill "provides that a group or individual policy of accident and health insurance or managed care plan amended, delivered, issued, or renewed after the amendatory Act shall provide coverage for the treatment of pediatric autoimmune neuropsychiatric disorders associated with streptococcal infections and acute-onset neuropsychiatric syndrome, including but not limited to the use of intravenous immunoglobulin therapy (IVIG). Effective immediately." (http://openstates.org/il/bills/looth/ HB2721/) The bill was passed in both the Senate and the House with overwhelming bipartisan support. The Illinois State Medical Society was also a proponent of the bill.

I love that Charlie's Law was started by two moms. They joined forces when their sons began showing signs of severe mental illness following strep throat infections. The law was named after both women's sons.

Charlie Drury came down with strep throat on his eighth birthday. Following the infection, Charlie developed extreme OCD, anxiety, anorexia, and hallucinations. Kate Drury paid $12,000 out of pocket for her son's IVIG treatment. The experience made her think of other families who could not afford treatment. She teamed up with Wendy Nawara. Together they worked on a legislation to make Illinois the first (and at the time of this writing, only) state to require insurance providers to cover the cost of IVIG treatment for PANDAS/PANS. Senator Tom Cullerton introduced the bill. Four years later, Governor Bruce Rauner signed Charlie's Law at the Drury's kitchen table.

Insurance providers, never underestimate the power of a mom fighting for her child. I am forever grateful to Kate Drury and Wendy Nawara for using their experiences to give other families the chance for treatment.

After the scheduled call between Dr. K and the doctor for the insurance company, I made another call to the insurance.

"It's still showing denied. Is there anything else I can—"

"I'm sure you're aware of House Bill 2721?" I interjected.

A full thirty seconds of dead silence followed. I let it hang. "Um, no, ma'am, I'm not familiar."

Right, I thought. "Well, House Bill 2721 was passed into law on June 18, 2017. It legally requires private insurance companies to provide treatment for PANDAS, including IVIG. My son is diagnosed with PANDAS, so it's actually illegal for the insurance company to deny coverage for this procedure."

Another several seconds of silence followed. "Oh, ma'am, don't worry, I'm sure we can get this worked out for you."

"Thank you. I'd appreciate that, as we will take this further if we need to. The insurance company is breaking the law by denying coverage."

"Please don't worry, ma'am. We'll get it worked out for you."

I hung up, vindicated.

The peer-to-peer consult between Dr. K and the insurance company's doctor was scheduled for September 10. Ten days later, I received a letter in the mail dated September 11, 2019. "We received a request to review outpatient services for you. Based on information submitted, we have determined that the IVIG treatment is medically necessary."

32

EXODUS

The Lord is not slow in keeping his promises, as some
understand slowness. Instead, he is patient with you, not wanting
anyone to perish, but everyone to come to repentance.

—2 Peter 3:9

September 25, 2019–October 3, 2019

The night before the IVIG procedure we were on pins and needles.
Yet I felt a sense of peace beyond understanding. We had Lorraine
lined up to stay with TJ until a neighbor picked him up from school.
Lorraine thought we were wrong for putting Jack through the procedure, and she questioned whether we'd done our research. She was
frosty with us when she arrived the morning of the procedure.

"Can't she just be supportive?" I whispered to Luke as we pulled
out of the garage.

"Don't let her get to you, hun," Luke said. You got the insurance company to cover the procedure. We've been fighting this for so
long. Let's focus on getting him better."

I admired Luke's ability to compartmentalize. He was right.
Lorraine and I would ultimately work out our differences and she'd
come to understand.

I turned toward the backseat. "How are you doing, Jack?"

"He yawned. "Okay. Tired. Scared for the IV."

"I know sweetie," I said, again wishing I could do it for him. "It'll be over soon."

"What would you like for lunch, bud?" Luke asked. "I can run out and get something this afternoon."

I had to smile. The sun was just rising, turning the sky from gray to a more palatable pink.

"I don't know," Jack said. "We'll see what's around there."

The majority of the drive was quiet, each of us lost in our own thoughts.

"Look, hunny, there's a Starbucks right there," Luke said as we turned off the main road. "I can walk over and get us some once Jack is settled."

I nodded. We pulled up to the one-story red brick building. Only a few other cars dotted the parking lot. I gave Jack a squeeze as we walked down the tiled hallway.

We came to varnished cherry wood double doors with glass in the center. Jack pushed the silver button that caused the doors to open. The surgical suite was spacious, bright, and modern. I had a fleeting moment of uncertainty as I checked Jack in. Was I wrong in putting him through this? Would it be too traumatic? I paused signing the consent forms. I'm sure every parent who takes their child in for a medical procedure goes through this. It felt counterintuitive, putting my child through pain—signing my permission. I recalled the daily Bible verse that had popped up on my phone that morning. "The Lord is not slow in keeping His promises, as some understand slowness. Instead, He is patient with you, not wanting anyone to perish, but everyone to come to repentance" (1 Peter 3:9). I signed the forms.

We didn't have to wait at all before going back. A kind nurse in mint green scrubs adorned with white cats gave Luke and I white netlike gowns to put over our clothes and matching booties to put over our shoes. The surgical center was clean. We were led to a small curtained-off room. The rooms were separated by plexiglass walls. The little boy in the adjacent room was crying. Jack looked at me, wide-eyed. I gave him what I hoped was a reassuring smile.

"Okay, Jack, you can take your shoes off and get comfortable. Here's a gown for you." The nurse patted the white gown at the foot of the bed—which looked more like an oversized recliner than a hospital bed. "You can leave your bottoms on. I'll give you a minute."

We helped Jack into his gown and got him settled in bed. Luke extracted our giant bottle of alkaline water and set it on the rolling table near the foot of the bed. A small stack of Styrofoam cups was already on the otherwise empty table.

The nurse returned with another jug of water and two small plastic cups, one half-filled with clear liquid and the other filled to the top with cherry-red liquid. "Are you from Illinois?" the nurse asked.

"Yes," Luke said.

"Oh, well that's good. A lot of our patients come from far away."

I thought about my struggle getting the insurance to cover the procedure. With our deductible, we ended up paying close to $3,000, which was $9,000 less than what we would've paid without coverage. I thought of the families who travelled from far away and the cost they faced. I said a prayer of thanks to God for his provisions and prayed for other families finding treatment for their children.

If you research PANDAS or ask many medical professionals, they'll tell you that it's rare. Yet there were three other boys at the surgical center, and Dr. K performs IVIG every day. Is it rare or unrecognized?

"All right, Jack, I'm going to give you some Tylenol and a double-dose of Benadryl to start."

Jack scrunched up his nose. "Will it taste bad?"

The nurse held up the red liquid. "I don't think so. It should taste like cherries."

"You've had these medicines before, Jack," I said. "It shouldn't be too bad. Just drink it down in one shot."

"Teaching him how to do shots already?" Luke smiled at me, trying to lighten the mood as always. I tried to manage a smile.

"Also, will he get the numbing cream?" I pointed to my hand.

"Yes, absolutely. I'll be right back with that." Her crocks squeaked on the linoleum floor as she walked away.

Jack grew pale. "Mom? Dad? I'm scared for the needle."

"I know, bud. The hard part will be over soon," Luke said.

"It'll be okay, Jack. Mom and Dad are here. Why don't we watch something to try and get your mind off it?"

"Okay."

I fished my phone out of my backpack, positioned myself by Jack's head, and put on his favorite YouTube channel. Within a minute, he was laughing. He stopped abruptly when the nurse returned. She tapped his hand and then his arm, looking for a vein. Jack began to cry softly. I rubbed his back.

"Oh, it's okay, hunny. This is just the numbing spray. It feels a little cold. Okay?"

Jack nodded bravely. She sprayed his arm and his hand.

Before we knew it, she was back with a tourniquet, a needle, and another middle-aged nurse in carnation pink scrubs. I crawled onto the bed between Jack and the wall. I brought his snuggle blankie and his stuffed Minecraft iron golem up near his face. Jack cried softly. I felt near tears myself, but I pushed them back and whispered reassuring words to Jack.

The nurse wrapped the tourniquet around Jack's arm and asked him to make a fist. She tapped his hand. "One, two, three."

The needle broke the skin. Jack screamed some choice words he'd unfortunately already learned from other kids.

"Shh, shh." Luke rubbed Jack's hair. "We don't want to teach the boy next door a new word."

"It's not going in. Sorry, hunny." They had to stick Jack again. I wanted it to be over for him.

"You're doing great. I'm so proud of you." I asked Luke to hand me a cup of water. I brought it to Jack's lips. "Drink as much as you can."

They rolled in an IV pole. A glass jar with clear liquid that looked like gel with bubbles hung from it. This was the donor immunoglobulin that would restart Jack's immune system. They hooked it up to the tube coming from Jack's hand. The nurse fiddled with the tube and tapped the jar. "I can't get it started. Let me go get one of our other nurses and see if he can help us with this. Hang in there."

"Will they have to stick me again?" Jack's eyes filled with fresh tears.

"I don't know, sweetie. I hope not." I ached for him.

"Oh no! Oh no!"

The two women returned with a burly man in black scrubs. He snapped on blue gloves. "Let's see what's going on here."

Jack cried softly while the man jiggled the IV tube, tapped the jar, and checked the IV site. "No, it's not in the vein. Sorry, buddy."

"No, not again!" Jack shrieked.

"Can you give him something to calm him?" I asked. "This is traumatic for him."

"I know," the woman in the pink scrubs said sympathetically. "I'm very sorry, but Dr. K doesn't like for us to give sedatives. The Benadryl will make him sleepy. Jose here will do it. He's the best."

"Thank you, my dear." He slid the needle out of Jack's hand and searched for a vein. "Tiny veins."

After what seemed like an hour but was probably only a minute, he found a vein higher up on Jack's arm near his shoulder. I held Jack as close as I could. He screamed. Finally, it was over.

"It's in," Jose said. He opened the valve and the liquid began to flow. "Beautiful."

I wiped Jack's tears. Luke brought him a tissue. "You did great, sweetie," I said. "It's all over. They won't have to stick you again."

"They had to stick me three times!" Jack moaned.

I looked at Luke. "I know. I'm sorry it was so tough. Now you can relax and watch your videos. Just think, you would be in school right now."

"I'd rather be in school." Jack's eyes had begun to glaze over.

"You can take a little nap if you want." I brought the white blanket up under Jack's arms.

"Can I watch YouTube for a while?"

"Of course." I handed him my phone.

"Why don't you have a seat, sweetie." Luke gestured toward the upholstered chair against the plexiglass wall. "I'll walk over and get us some Starbucks."

I gave Jack more water before settling into the chair with my notebook. It was hard to write, though. I couldn't get the sound of Jack screaming out of my mind.

Luke returned with a macchiato for me, a black coffee for himself, and a cheese Danish for Jack. The hours ticked by. Jack was sleepy and calm, but he didn't nap. I read him his science and history chapters. I'm not sure he absorbed any of it. Mostly, I let him watch videos. He deserved it.

Luke balanced his computer on his lap and tried to work. I vacillated between giving Jack water and trying to write. Around eleven o'clock, Jack said he was hungry.

"What do you have a taste for, bud?"

Jack yawned. "I don't know. Maybe burgers."

"Sounds good." Luke looked at his phone. "There's a Culvers about five minutes from here."

A few minutes after Luke left, I heard Dr. K's Croatian accent next door.

"Are you gonna take my blood?" the little boy next to us asked.

"No way," Dr. K said. "We're going to give you some magic stuff to help."

Dr. K came to see us next. "Hello, Mary Lou." He squeezed Jack's knee and then turned to shake my hand. "How're we doing?"

"Pretty good, I think." My phone buzzed. "Let me see that for a minute, Jack. I need to see if it's TJ's school." I checked the screen. "Excuse me, I need to take this."

"Sure, go ahead. No worries."

"Hello?" I said into the phone.

"Hello, Mrs. Shepherd?"

"Yes."

"This is Dr. Chu."

Dr. Chu was TJ's occupational therapist at school. "Yes, hello. Can you hear me? I'm at the doctor."

"Oh, do you need me to let you go?"

"No. I can talk."

Luke walked back into the room and greeted Dr. K. I pointed to my phone and exited the surgical suite, retreating to a quiet, sunny atrium in the center of the building.

"I just saw TJ," Dr. Chu was saying. "His hand-eye coordination is improving. We've been playing catch with a balloon to boost his confidence. He was able to button a shirt by himself. He was so proud. It was cute. I'll send you the video."

"Thank you." I paced between the small trees.

"I've also been observing him in the classroom. I spoke to Ms. Jacobs, and we are seeing some of what you mentioned with the distractibility, inattention, and sensory seeking. For instance, he's been chewing on his sleeve. Ms. Jacobs says he's quiet in class but compliant, although easily distracted by noises and his peers moving around. Sometimes Ms. Jacobs puts folders up on his desk to block out some of the stimuli. We'll keep an eye on it."

"Thank you." I liked Dr. Chu and TJ's entire special education team. I was grateful for our experience at his school. I was also admittedly floundering a bit, wondering for the millionth time how parents juggled the needs of multiple kids, especially on the special needs front. It was a little overwhelming, speaking to a therapist about one child's needs while at a medical procedure with the other. It was good, though; they were both getting what they needed.

Dr. Chu and I talked for a few more minutes about TJ's processing speed and the likely addition of ADHD to his diagnosis before I returned to Luke and Jack and my lunch.

Jack was sleepy for the remainder of the day. They taped up his IV before we left. We picked TJ up on our way home Jack rested on the couch for the rest of the day. We got takeout from his favorite Asian restaurant.

The following morning, I took Jack back to the surgical center while Luke stayed behind to drive TJ to school before meeting us. Dr. K and the nurses greeted us enthusiastically and set us up in "our" area. The nurse gave Jack Benadryl and Tylenol as well as an extra pillow and blanket and extra water. I set Jack up with his snuggle blankie and golem and gave him water.

"When's Dad getting here?" Jack asked.

I checked the time. "It's a little after seven now. He'll drop TJ off at eight fifteen, and then he'll head over."

The nurse returned and hung the next jar of immunoglobulin. "Will it hurt?" Jack asked.

The nurse smiled. "Not at all, sweetie. No stick today. I'm just going to flush your tube out and hang this up."

The remainder of the IVIG infusion was uneventful. Jack recovered at home over the next ten days. On day five he developed a bad headache and threw up despite his increased fluid intake. We treated it with ibuprofen, Benadryl, and lots of alkaline water. By day ten, Jack was back to school and back to himself. Once again, Jack healed, and Luke and I clung to hope.

33

THIRTY-THREE DAYS AFTER

Moses answered the people, "Do not be afraid. Stand firm
and you will see the deliverance the Lord will bring you today.
The Egyptians you see today you will never see again."
—Exodus 14:13

October 30, 2019

Thirty-three days post IVIG, Jack had a flare. He'd been himself up
until that day.

It's heartbreaking to watch Jack suffer. It's a helpless feeling as
a parent, not being able to make the monsters go away. I hope. God
promised to heal Jack. I know that. I don't know when. I am David
crying out to God in Psalms. "How much longer, Lord?"

We are the Israelites in the desert. We did what God said. We
crossed the Red Sea and here we are in the desert. We believe, but we
lament, as humans do.

That day, homeschooling was a challenge. We started our day
playing "Mrs. Antbottom." It's usually a good sign when Jack wants
to play that—to engage. Jack's was reading more, of his own volition.
I was cracking down on the screen time limits. There were tears from
both boys, but Jack was placated when he learned he could earn extra
screen time by doing extra chores, completing extra credit assignments, or reading beyond what's assigned for school. The result was

more reading and less time on his computer. He wasn't even asking to "cash in" his extra reading. I had reason to have faith.

But the day before Halloween, he struggled. His geography class requires memorization of countries and capitals and their placement on a map. Fifth grade highlighted Jack's struggles with working memory and executive functioning. Before I understood PANDAS, I believed Jack was using selective memory and conveniently forgetting when I asked him to do something, gave him a warning, or asked him to reiterate what we'd learned for school. Sometimes, maybe, it is? It can be difficult to tell. But during a recent lecture I watched of Dr. K's, he mentioned children not being able to recall something just asked and a lightbulb went off. I saw it firsthand that day. We studied his map of South America. After two hours of map games and going over and over the countries quizzing him, he could rattle them off. After lunch, however, the information seemed to be just…gone. The same thing happened when I made flashcards with the countries on one side and capitals on the other. We ran through them four or five at a time. I showed Jack the country then flipped the card over to show and say the capital. Then I quizzed Jack. Once he mastered a group, I took out a card or two and replaced it with a new one. By the time I cycled back through those four or five cards, he'd forgotten the ones he'd mastered only a minute before. This may not sound out of the ordinary for a fifth-grade boy, but seven hours of repetition made it was clear nothing was sticking.

I saw the flare coming. Over the years, I've become fluent in my ability to detect the subtle signs, much like my experience of visual disturbances and upper back pain preceding my headaches. Both events most often prove as easy to halt as an oncoming train. For my monster migraines, I've been advised to avoid stress. Does any human being actually believe this is possible? For Jack, I can try to limit his exposure to germs, support his immune system, and monitor his diet and sleep hygiene. But the flares come, most often on the heels of an illness. Exposure to environmental irritants, chlorine, and consumption of food dye also serve as triggers.

Dr. K laid out the path to remission, and we followed it: removal of Jack's tonsils and adenoids followed by IVIG treatment, and antibiotic therapy beginning one week prior to the procedure and continuing for a year after. Jack had his tonsils removed April 15, 2019. He had a flare on April 10, during which he was throwing things, back talking, refusing to do his homework, and exhibiting motor and vocal tics. By April 20, he'd stopped holing himself up in his room with his computer. Light returned to his eyes. His mood was better, his irritability was essentially gone, and he was engaging in creative play as well as schoolwork. During this reprieve, Jack was able to describe his flares to us, from the inside.

"It feels like I should be able to control myself, but I can't," he told me. "It's like I'm in a dream, and I'm watching my body do these things and telling it to stop, but it won't, and I can't make it. Then I just feel so bad. I don't know why I act like that."

For years, we didn't know either. When I thought back on the ways I tried to get through to Jack, the times I reacted out of desperation, anger, and fear, the night I yelled, "What is wrong with you?" I felt sick. If I let myself go down that rabbit hole, I could fill these pages with my ignorance and my failures. I own those mistakes, but at the end of the day I have to forgive myself. I'm not saying it's easy; it's a daily process of actively choosing to live today with no regrets and forgive myself for my lack of understanding. I didn't know what I didn't know.

I'm writing these pages because other parents out there right now are lost, confused, angry, and desperate. They are searching for help and colliding with closed doors at every turn. They are trying stricter parenting, and they are giving in, sometimes on the same day. They're losing their children over and over again without understanding how or why, or how to protect them. They don't know what happened. When Jack was three, I thought he hated me; I thought I had failed him, and I thought he wanted to hurt people on purpose. If that sounds dramatic, it's because it is. It was. It seemed every day was a battle ground. If I'd read a book like this when Jack was first taken, it may have opened my eyes to another possibility. My child was sick. Not mentally (although that was the result) but physically. Our child's brain was being attacked by his immune system, and we were using behavior modification. We were coming at a forest fire with a squirt gun, and not even the right type of squirt gun.

Don't misunderstand; therapy is an invaluable part of the healing process. Jack needs treatment as a whole. He needed to learn the deescalation skills. We needed those psych evals to give us a roadmap, even if we took several wrong turns. Now, regardless of the results of the IVIG, Jack needs therapy to build up the skills he lost to the repeated attacks on his brain. At ten and a half, Jack struggled to tie his shoes, open a bottle of water, and even use utensils adequately. Jack is very open, but he'll acknowledge none of these things, which makes sense. I had developmental delays as a child, and I remember being teased when I needed the teacher to tie my shoe or open my can of pop. Fortunately, Jack hasn't been ridiculed for these things. But I fear they will impact his confidence.

But I'm procrastinating writing about the flare. On the way home from TJ's social group I told Jack he and I could watch a show together after he completed his work. Luke offered to work with Jack when we got home. He was surprised at how little Jack retained from studying. Jack reiterated his apathy for the test, and all things learning. This was the wrong this to say to his ambitious and driven father. Luke launched into his spiel about the importance of learning, working hard in school, and having goals, and providing someday. Jack responded to this by throwing a pair of plastic Halloween glasses at Luke. This resulted in Luke yelling and Jack storming to his room.

Well, I'd dealt with some behaviors from TJ that afternoon and I'd suggested to Luke that maybe we gave in too much. But when I saw Jack storm up to his room. I knew he was done. I should have pulled the plug on the homework then and there. Instead, I told Jack to take a ten-minute silent reading break in his room, after which I sent him back downstairs to apologize and finish his geography with Luke while I bathed TJ and got him to bed.

Once TJ was asleep, I forced myself out of his bed and back to the frontlines, wondering if the day would ever reach its conclusion. Jack was calmly mastering a geography challenge on my computer. Outwardly, everything was fine. Jack got as far as possible on his studying. I went over grammar with him and asked him to get ready for bed. He kept wandering back downstairs still dressed.

"Jack, how are you still up at ten o'clock on a school night?" Luke said.

"He had a lot of work," I supplied. Luke's look alerted me to the "helpfulness" of my answer to his rhetorical question.

Ten minutes later, Jack came down in his red and blue flannel pajama pants and announced he was ready for bed. "Can we watch now, Mom?"

Earlier in the day, I'd promised him we'd watch a show together once he'd completed his assignments. It was late, but it was a twenty-minute show if we fast-forwarded the commercials. Jack was pacing, clicking his tongue, and wide-eyed. Don't ask me why I thought the rest of his work would conclude any earlier. I figured an extra twenty minutes to wind down would actually get him to sleep earlier. The rage was boiling just under the surface, and I could see it. I looked at Luke.

His eyes were steely, and his jaw was set. My own father exhibited the exact look when he'd made a final, iron-clad decision. "It's ten twenty at night. You can't watch a show at ten twenty at night," Luke said.

We cut the wrong wire. The tears were instant, "Mom promised!" Jack wailed.

I know by now any statement is a promise to Jack. "I did tell him we could watch it after he finished his work, since he worked all day," I said.

Luke gestured at the clock hanging above the archway separating the kitchen from the family room. "It's ten twenty at night. You can't watch TV with him at ten twenty at night."

If he says "ten twenty at night" one more time I'm going to lose it, I thought. "I'm sorry, Jack, I didn't realize how late it would get. We'll watch it tomorrow. Besides, tomorrow's a new episode. We can have a double feature!" My voice was shrill, desperate false cheer barely masking my dread.

Jack's eyes widened. "You promised! You're a liar!"

"Now you're calling your mother a liar?" Luke said.

"I did tell him we could—"

"It's almost ten thirty on a school night."

"I know what time it is," I exploded. "I actually can tell time."

"Dad's mean! He's ruining our night! He ruins everything," Jack yelled over us.

Okay, obviously, Luke and I needed to present a united front. But my every instinct was to pump the brakes on this meltdown. If I could have a do-over, I'd tell Jack Dad and I would talk about it, but he needed to calm down. I'd take Luke into our bedroom and explain my reasoning. He'd explain his and we'd come to a mutual decision to present to Jack. That all looks really good on paper. That's not what either of us did.

"Dad says it's too late," I told Jack.

"I don't care what Dad says."

"You have to. He's your father."

"I don't. He's mean."

"I'm mean? I just helped you with your homework and you threw glasses at me and didn't even apologize."

I'd assumed Jack had apologized like I'd requested. Regardless, things were quickly unraveling. We were all exhausted, and I didn't even want to think about Halloween the next day. I'd never cared less about the capital of El Salvador. If anyone from San Salvador happens to read this, nothing personal.

I ascended the stairs and focused on making my voice soothing and nonconfrontational. It came out more pleading. "Jack, honey, we're all tired. Let's just get ready for—"

"I'm NOT tired," Jack screamed. "Let's go upstairs and watch the show in your room."

I followed Jack up the stairs. "Come on, Jack, let's lay down and read."

"No! We're watching the show."

"Okay, that's it, you're going to bed." Luke called.

I turned toward the muted pounding of Luke's feet on the carpeted stairs. "I got it."

He huffed down the hall to our bedroom. "Fine."

It wasn't clear if he was more frustrated with me or Jack by this point.

Jack darted down the hallway in pursuit of Luke. I followed Jack.

"I want to watch the show. I want to watch the show. I want to watch the show."

Luke spun around. "I'm going to bed, Jack."

I reached for Jack's arm in a last-ditch attempt at keeping the plane in the air. "We're all going to bed, Jack. Come on. Let's lay in bed and read *Whatshisface*," I said, referring to the current Gordon Korman book we were reading.

"I want to watch the show. I was looking forward to it all day. We couldn't watch it last night because it got too late. I worked hard all day so we could watch it. It's my favorite thing to do together. We were going to have our night together and it's ruined." Jack dissolved into heaving sobs.

Man, he could really work at the guilt-trip travel agency. I gave Luke a pleading look.

He shook his head. "You were just telling me that we need to stop giving in."

"You're right, it's just I was referring more to TJ and his behavior lately. I feel like he doesn't take us seriously when we allow him to earn back privileges."

"I want to watch it! You promised. It's ruined." We were beyond salvation. Jack bolted for the stairs. "I'm going to watch it downstairs, so Dad won't know," he announced.

I lunged for Jack, anticipating the difficulty of getting him back upstairs. But he was already propelling himself down at such a rate I was afraid he'd fall.

"Jack, if you go down those stairs, you'll lose it for tomorrow," Luke called.

I pursued Jack downstairs and into the family room, where he threw himself on the couch and simultaneously snatched the remote in a death grip.

I wrestled it away from him. I attempted to put my weight on him and slow his racing body and brain. I tried to take him in my arms like he was little again. I tried to wrench him back from the abductor. What happens when a mother's arms aren't enough for comfort? When hugs are met with blows? *It's not him, it's not him, it's not him.*

"I'm disappointed too, Jack. I didn't realize how long everything would take. But's it's not going anywhere. I won't watch it without you."

"Let's just watch it now. Dad won't know."

"Jack, Dad and I are on the same team. Dad said it's too late. Now let's go upstairs." My back protested as I tried to haul him of the couch. "Ouch! Jack, that's enough. I can't do this with you. You're not getting the show. Your options are to lay in bed while I read or keep screaming. I enjoy reading with you."

After another few rounds of "you promised, Dad ruined the night, he's so mean, I want to watch it," Luke got involved again.

He entered the family room, his body rigid with frustration and exhaustion. "You're keeping me up. You're going to wake your brother."

"This isn't helping him get to bed sooner," I muttered, lamenting on the fact that the stupid show would've been over already.

Luke glared at me. "Nice, Hope."

"Just go to bed, it doesn't affect you," Jack said, writhing away from Luke.

"I can't go to sleep because you're screaming."

"I'll let you sleep if you say I can watch the show. Otherwise, I'll keep screaming."

"Jack—" I tried.

"That's it. You're going to bed." Luke attempted to lift Jack's ninety-pound body of the couch.

Jack flailed like he was being kidnapped. Which he was, just not by his father.

Will this night ever end? I thought. "Luke, let me handle this. This isn't helping. We need to deescalate."

"Don't use buzzwords with me, Hope."

I recognized the mode he was in because I'm in it too often myself. The why-can't-the-rules-of-regular-parenting-apply mode.

"We made an agreement that when one of us is getting too frustrated and yelling, the other steps in." Luke's done that for me countless times. When parenting gets extreme it's helpful to tap out.

"You told me we need to be firmer!" Luke continued trying to wrestle Jack off the couch.

"Why are you yelling at me? I don't deserve to be yelled at."

"You keep saying, 'Dad says it's too late,' trying to make me the bad guy!"

"I'm backing you! I'm telling him he needs to respect what you say."

I felt like Luke was exploding over what I had dealt with all day. I felt he was changing my plan to handle the night with a very burned out and stressed-out Jack. I didn't tell him any of that until after the storm.

"Just go to bed." I grabbed Luke's arm and guided him away from the couch. "I'll get him to bed."

Luke threw up his hands. "Fine." He retreated.

After several more unsuccessful attempts to cajole, demand, and pull Jack up to his room, I gave up. "I guess you'll sleep down here. I'm going to bed."

Jack let out a glass-shattering shriek and followed me to the stairs screaming that he wanted to watch the show. He planted himself four steps from the top while I closed ours and TJ's bedroom doors. I returned to the top of the stairs where Jack's room was. It's my favorite room in the house. I'd adorned it with soft Christmas-type lights, a diffuser, a bean bag chair, a fuzzy grey shag rug, family pictures, and books. When Jack saw me, he scrambled down a few more stairs.

"Okay. I'm going to lay in your bed. Come in when you're ready for me to read."

I'm not sure how long Jack sat on the staircase screaming. I was afraid he'd wake TJ or continue to keep Luke awake. If I could just get Jack into his room…

This will end at some point, I told myself, as I always do when a meltdown happens. The only course of action is to keep everyone safe and wait it out. Eventually, Jack couldn't resist coming into the room to continue begging me for the show. I got up and shut the door. Confining him was my best option.

"Come on, Jack," I coaxed, "Let's read."

I guided him to the bed, positioning myself on the edge so that Jack was between me and the wall. I covered us with his comforter. I began our chapter, hoping beyond hope that the story would draw him in. I put extra inflection into the Shakespearean language of the sixteenth century ghost character, modifying my volume along with Jack's. The soundtrack in my house that night included a lot of exaggerated annunciations "verily" followed by screams of, "I want to watch the show!" Jack quieted periodically, and I read on, my animated voice contrasting the tension in every single muscle. *Please, please, please be over*, I thought.

But each silence was followed by banging on the wall and screaming louder and louder until his voice got horse. Instead of calming, Jack's agitation increased. My heart sank, but I was not surprised.

Jack sprang onto his feet on the mattress. I abandoned the book, rose to my knees, and tried to lay Jack back down. When my kids were babies and toddlers resisting naps, they would make their bodies rigid and lock their limbs. Jack was doing that, except now his body was ninety pounds. I felt the regrettable twinge in my back as Jack wrenched away from me and scrambled out of bed. Anticipating his next move, I lunged for the door, and just as I had so many times before, barricaded it with my body. I could feel my resolve crumbling. Exhausted, I curled up in front of the door. I hadn't noticed the dog was in the room. He curled up against me.

Jack's face looked blue in the soft glow of the nightlight. "No, you're not going to sleep! I'm going to be stubborn! You lied, and I won't let you go to sleep until you let me watch the show!"

For the millionth time I wondered if any of this was in Jack's control. I looked at him. His body was rigid, vibrating with rage. He poked at me around the dog, who adjusted his body as a barrier between us. It wasn't Jack. No, I don't believe he was in control. I was desperate to snap him out of it.

I just want this to be over, I thought. I wanted more than just an end to this particular meltdown. I wanted an end to PANDAS, and I wouldn't let go of the belief that it was coming. I dreamt of experiencing the typical phases—middle school, budding independence, even puberty. Puberty with all its smells, changes, and hormones, would be a breeze after PANDAS. I don't know if I'll ever fully let go of the sadness about the losses throughout Jack's childhood, but I will fully appreciate every moment PANDAS doesn't steal. *It's almost over. I won't lose hope. I won't lose faith. I won't lose Jack.*

Sometimes I can shock Jack out of his trance. It's always a last-ditch attempt. I admit it's often more about me reaching the end of my resolve, but this time, well maybe it was partially that and partially planned to snap him back.

"Jack—"

"No! I won't let you go to sleep! Let me watch the show!"

"Jack," I raised my voice to be heard over his, "you're almost eleven years old. You are not an infant. You don't keep your parents up all night."

I hate when I say things like this. I never want my harsh words ringing in my children's heads. But Jack's face changed in that moment, and my stomach unclenched. When Jack snaps out of his rages, he literally deflates. His shoulders dropped, his eyes widened, and his head dropped.

"I'm sorry," he cried, his tears of rage flowing into tears of remorse. He crawled into bed, clutched his blanket and sloth, and repeated his apology.

Alarmed, Pavlov went over to Jack's bed and tried to shove his nose under the comforter, tail wagging uncertainly. I pulled my stiff body off the floor and returned to Jack's bed. I rubbed his back.

"It's okay," I soothed.

"I don't know why I act like this."

"It's not your fault."

"I'm a bad person." Jack's voice was muffled by the blanket.

My heart wrenched, and for the millionth time, I wondered if my response was correct or dead wrong. "It's not you, it's PANDAS. You will get better. We love you and you're a good boy."

Should I be sharing all this PANDAS information with him? Will he embrace it as his identity? Do I, as his previous counselor suggested, "Talk about mental health stuff too much"? Am I giving him more information than he can handle? Will he feel PANDAS is an excuse for his behavior? But isn't it? Not an excuse, maybe, but an explanation.

I can never untell Jack what I've shared. I don't know if I'm right or wrong, but I have to do what I feel is right. I didn't understand my depression and anxiety growing up. I didn't understand why I felt sad all the time, like there was a cloud following me that didn't plague other eight-year-olds. I didn't understand why my stomach got sick every day before school, and the nausea persisted until the final bell rang. I didn't understand why I missed thirty days of second grade when doctors couldn't find anything wrong with my stomach. Nothing was wrong with my stomach, but there was something different in my head. I don't think not knowing was better because I knew I was different.

Anyway, Jack and I talked and prayed. We reminded ourselves to trust God's promises. I finished reading the chapter and even got a few laughs out of Jack. *Thank you, Gordon Korman.* I stayed in Jack's bed for a while, watching him sleep, hoping his dreams were calm. I replayed the entire meltdown and events leading up to it, picking apart my every word and decision of the day and night.

I shouldn't have promised him he could watch the show after completing his work. Well, okay, I didn't say those words, but I should've known Jack would hear a promise. I should've started the school day earlier. I should've taken Luke aside and explained my reasoning for wanting to allow Jack the show. Maybe I should've let the geography test go. Indeed, it was difficult to care about a quiz in the face of a PANDAS rage. But PANDAS and it's resulting executive functioning deficits and difficulty completing assignments, made me worry about where Jack was academically, and whether I was letting him fall behind. It's a tough balance. Guilt is rough.

We want so badly to give our kids the absolute best—the best of ourselves, the best of themselves, the best of life. But we don't have a crystal ball. I never would've imagined the issues I'd face when

Jack was growing under my heart. Obviously. I expected the struggles and joys. I even worried about accidents, natural disasters, and kidnappings. I didn't worry that my child would be kidnapped without leaving the house. I didn't expect the trauma and heartbreak of being attacked by someone barely resembling your child. I didn't anticipate the soaring joy of a typical moment, the clinging to the shiny calm between storms. I never imagined my own strength, growing instead of waning each time I'm up against a wall of resistance in the form of an insurance company with a god complex, disbelieving doctors, counselors, and those in our personal life, ignorance, and obstacles. I won't stop with Jack. When Jack was diagnosed with autism, PANDAS was something I'd heard of but all I knew was that it was an acronym for some vague medical thing. If not for Charlotte, I may have plodded along with inefficient tools indefinitely. I'm grateful every day for her, and to God for putting her in my path.

I returned to our room sometime near midnight.

"I'm sorry," Luke's soft voice said in the dark. "I should've listened to you. But you said you wanted us to be firmer and then you wanted to give in, and I was confused."

In my exhausted ears, Luke's explanation negated his apology. "It's fine," I said in that way we women do when it is absolutely not fine.

I finished getting ready and crawled into bed, my body heavy and my mind foggy. "I feel like every situation and kid is different. I was referring specifically to TJ and our habit of giving him second and third chances to earn back privileges. I just knew Jack was burned out. I know from myself, when I'm doing things around the house or with the kids right up to bedtime, I have to watch a show, read, or do something mindless to wind down or I can't sleep. I figured another twenty minutes would actually get him to sleep sooner."

"It turned out you were right. He was up after eleven. I feel bad that I yelled, but you said we have to be firmer."

"This situation was different. I saw this meltdown coming." My burn-out was making me terse.

"You kept saying, 'Dad said no,' trying to make me the bad guy."

"Luke, we've always stepped in, when one of us is getting burned out and starting to yell, the other steps in to deescalate." I paused. "You're right, part of me was trying to make you the bad guy."

"I understand." Luke was quiet for a moment. "He never apologized for throwing the glasses at me. I didn't think he should get rewarded for his behavior."

I was taken aback. "I thought when I sent Jack downstairs you guys dealt with that. I thought he'd apologized."

"Nope."

"Well, when I came downstairs, he was calmly doing the computer game and you were on the couch."

"I was helping him. I went over the countries with him and then had him work on the game. He was doing well."

"Okay, well, I'm sorry, from my observation everything was resolved. I felt like the show was a whole separate issue since I mentioned that on the way home from social group."

"I was really frustrated by his attitude and him throwing the glasses at me. He just doesn't care."

"I know. I was dealing with that stuff all day. I hate hearing him say he doesn't care, but after talking to him, I feel like he's saying he doesn't care in case he doesn't do well. I think on some level he knows he's struggling to retain the information. It's easier for him to say he doesn't care."

Luke was quiet for so long I thought he'd fallen asleep. "I feel really horrible about how the night went, and yelling."

"I feel bad too."

"It's over and done with."

"I never want to make him feel bad. It's not his fault."

"I know. Me too."

Then we cried together in the darkness, as we had so many nights before. But this time I had something different. Hope.

34

⤬

CURED

"In the days to come when your son asks you, 'What does this mean?' say to him, 'With a mighty hand the Lord brought us out of Egypt, out of the land of slavery.'"
—Exodus 13:14

November 2019–October 2020

After that brief flare, the changes in Jack were remarkable. He was, according to the terminology I'd learned on the PANDAS board, back to baseline. The boy who'd struggled to write a sentence in fifth grade was writing five-paragraph papers on his own. The rages were gone, and the sweetness was back. It's difficult to describe the gratitude, relief, hope, and euphoria of getting your lost child back. "Rejoice with me; I have found my lost sheep" (Luke 15:6).

Gone were the days of Jack hiding in his room. He interacted with us. Jack played outside and did his homework. Of course, we'd had these reprieves before. The time with Jack was sweet, and we savored it. Inevitably, though, the kidnapper swept the rug out from under us—swept our little boy out with the tide.

But as the months went on, we trusted more and more. I never completely stopped watching for the kidnapper, but one thing became clear as fall bled into winter and winter gave way to spring. We realized it slowly, insidiously—like a new mother realizing the pain of labor has passed and given way to new life. PANDAS was no longer controlling our lives.

*****

PANDAS had come into our lives suddenly, but it loosened its grip subtly. First, Jack gained more energy, like the life was flowing back into him. He started asking to go for walks. He smiled more and cried less and then rarely.

IVIG and the subsequent year of antibiotic and probiotic therapy did not, of course, turn Jack into the perfect child. It turned him back into *him*. I remember an afternoon four or five months after IVIG when Jack had a middle school tantrum over a paper, and I realized it wasn't a flare. Never has a parent felt that type of joy and gratitude over a child's tantrum.

Jack was assigned weekly five-paragraph papers. When he finished his paper, he brought it downstairs to me.

"There. Done," he said, thrusting the typed paper into my hand. "Can I play online with Owen now, please?"

"Hang on, let me check it over." As I read the paper, it became apparent that Jack had rushed through it, no doubt because Owen was online slaying zombies. It was full of abbreviated sentences and grammatical errors. Based on the detailed, articulate papers he'd been writing, I knew he could do better.

"Jack, you need to fix the mistakes I marked. I also want you to add more details to the body paragraphs. Don't rush through it or you'll have to do it again."

"Ugh, I didn't! Can I just go play with Owen, please?"

"After you do your paper, and no rushing. Like my dad always said, it's faster to take you time and do it right the first time."

"Oh my gosh!" My middle schooler snatched the paper back from me. "I can't believe you're making me do this again." He retreated upstairs to his computer.

My stomach knotted. After ten minutes of hearing Jack grumble, I went upstairs to see how the paper was going. He spun on his wobble stool when I came in.

"Mom, why didn't you like my paper?" He gave me an Emmy-worthy frown.

"I do like it, I just want more detail."

"That's so unfair, though. I want to play with Owen. He's waiting for me."

"The sooner you finish the sooner you can play. You're almost done. Clean it up and add a few sentences."

"Oh my gosh." Jack stomped his feet.

My stomach dropped to my feet. Jack began to cry. I looked at his eyes. They were clear. His pupils were normal. I also noticed he was trying to squeeze tears out. Without meaning to, I smiled.

"Why are you smiling?"

"Because you're stomping your feet over your paper."

"I'm not stomping *on* my paper." The corners of Jack's mouth turned up as he squeezed a few tears out. He giggled.

"Okay, silly. Do your paper." I practically danced out of his room.

Twenty minutes later Jack brought me a corrected paper. He happily returned upstairs to play with Owen.

"Two hours of screen time."

"I know, Mom."

It's worth mentioning the trauma response in parents of mentally ill children. With PANDAS specifically, you're living in a mine-field. You never know when the next attack will come. You don't know when your child will be snatched, and when or if they'll be returned. You live in a state of chronic hyper-vigilance, always prepared for battle. You can't exhale.

Living under constant threat takes a toll on you. I still watch Jack carefully. I still tense up when he gets irritable with me. Yet on that day Jack was being a typical middle schooler. I basked in the normalcy. Jack played with TJ and me. We had deep conversations. I got to know him again, and I was so proud of his resilient spirit.

We worked on healing Jack's brain and gut. In addition to five hundred milligrams of Augmentin, we gave him a multivitamin, Ester-C, fish oil, and probiotics daily. Jack had an extremely sensitive gag reflex, making it difficult for him to swallow the bitter antibiotic. The obvious first choice was liquid, but as soon as it hit the back of Jack's throat, he'd throw it back up. The pills were huge. We tried crushing them up and putting them in pudding then applesauce then yogurt. Finally, I bought gelatin capsules from the health food store. Luke crushed up the pills and funneled the powder into the capsules. Then Jack could swallow them with a spoon of applesauce.

Jack was seeing a new counselor—a thirty-something social worker named Seth. Jack related to him. They talked and joked a lot They developed a rapport. Seth also worked closely with me, bringing me into sessions as needed and asking me for weekly updates.

"You know," I told Seth during one of our earlier sessions, "we've been to a lot of therapists and you're the first one who doesn't make me feel like it's my fault."

"Really?"

I nodded.

"In my experience, the parents whose fault it is are not the parents who bring their kids to therapy."

Seth gave me a lot of peace with that statement.

Jack was doing well in therapy, at home, and in school. Our lives achieved a sense of normalcy we hadn't experienced in years. Then COVID-19 hit, showing further proof of God's perfect timing.

If COVID-19 had hit earlier, IVIG would've been unsafe or even impossible. We worried about Jack's immune system, but fortunately he'd been on antibiotics for six months. Dr. K said it would take a full year for the immune system to rebuild. Now I understand why God had placed the urgency in my heart. Only God knows the future and only He could see COVID-19 coming. He knew our window was closing, and we couldn't wait.

Both boys' schools scrambled to set up remote learning. TJ struggled without his special education in class services. His teacher was amazing as always. She set up bi-weekly read-a-louds for her class. At first, TJ was excited to see his teacher and classmates on the screen. Ultimately, online learning was too abstract for him, through no fault of the school.

Jack transitioned smoothly as his school set up a weekly zoom schedule. I struggled to keep track of the fluctuating times, but Jack took initiative.

"I don't need help, Mom," he told me.

Luke and I celebrated Jack's independence. At the beginning of the school year, I was sitting with Jack for upward of five hours attempting to guide him through a five-sentence paragraph. In March of fifth grade, he was finding zoom links, logging into class, and doing the majority of his assignments on his own. I can only imagine how we could've handled zoom classes and 100 percent at-home learning if PANDAS was still in the driver's seat. Even without COVID, I don't see how Jack would've gotten through fifth grade.

As I mentioned, we'd had reprieves before. This time felt different, and not only because it had been five months since Jack's last flare. Jack had never been this focused or independent on his schoolwork. He still struggled with depression, but it no longer seemed to control his life. Jack seemed to have matured several years in the span of a few months.

We slowed down with the world. My heart ached for those lost to the virus, and I worried what would happen if Jack were exposed, but I didn't mind staying home. In fact, it felt safe for me, holed up at home with my family.

COVID-19 brought about many changes. We were careful. If one of us needed to go to the store, we changed in the laundry room as soon as we walked in. I wiped down all groceries and packages with disinfecting wipes. When those could no longer be procured, I soaked baby wipes in hand sanitizer and made my own.

Not all of the changes were so cumbersome. Luke was working from home for the foreseeable future. Free from the hour plus commute into the city, he was able to spend more time with us and have dinner with us every night. We played more board games and watched more movies. For the first time in seven years, I felt at peace.

*****

Luke and I spent the eve of Jack's eleventh birthday constructing little plastic pinwheels in a variety of colors. When my soon-to-be eleven-year-old was in bed, I crept out to the front lawn and adorned the dark grass with colorful pinwheels. Near the sidewalk I placed a sign that read, "Happy Birthday, Jack 11 Love, Mom, Dad, and TJ." Finally, I tied a red and yellow happy birthday banner across the front porch. Jack was all smiles when he looked out the front window the next morning.

"Happy first day as an eleven-year-old!" I hugged Jack.

All birthdays are special, but Jack's eleventh birthday stood out. It was the first time since his third birthday that the kidnapper wasn't lurking in the shadows. It had been eight months since Jack had had a flare.

Luke and I stood in the kitchen smiling while Jack opened his present from us, my mom, and Luke's parents.

"Really?" He smiled up at us as he extracted the coveted gaming computer with its color changing fans.

It was an extravagant gift, but Jack had earned it. We were celebrating his return as much as his birthday. At 1:00 PM neighbors and friend pulled up in front of our house blaring their horns. Jack stood on the front lawn smiling broadly. Owen, Brooklyn, Xander, and Drew ran from their cars for some socially distanced pictures and conversation. Every birthday, Naomi, Adalyn, and I took what Naomi had dubbed "the three amigos" picture of Xander, Jack, and Owen followed by a picture of us three moms.

Jack showed so much maturity and understanding handling the disappointment of no party. We were also missing our tradition of letting the birthday person pick a restaurant for dinner. In Jack's case, this was always hibachi. He settled for chicken and rice takeout from his favorite Asian restaurant. It was the same meal he'd had the night of IVIG.

We hadn't seen anyone outside of family in three months and COVID was still a threat, but I decided to let Adalyn, Brooklyn, and Owen stay. All Jack wanted—I think even more than his computer—was to spend his birthday with his best friend and "girlfriend."

The kids played. The adults popped a bottle of champagne. Unfortunately, riots in our downtown area made it unsafe to pick up Jack's favorite takeout. He settled for pizza.

"Mommy?" Jack said as I tucked him in that night, "This is scary."

"I know, sweetie." We prayed for our country, and I snuggled him to sleep.

*****

We enjoyed a low-key, 1980s-like summer with no camps and classes and outdoor only playdates. As summer drew to a close, decision fatigue set in. Our public school district's plans vacillated between 100 percent online learning to a hybrid model and back again. With its small class sizes, Homeschool Haven was resuming its typical two day a week schedule.

After consulting with TJ's immensely helpful special education team and ensuring that he'd still get services virtually and speaking with TJ and Jack's counselors and Dr. K, we decided to send both boys to Homeschool Haven.

My friend Charlotte also decided to send her first-grader, Rick to HH. We were able to carpool. Charlotte took the kids in the mornings, and I picked them up in the afternoons. After school, Rick would stay at our house and play until dinner time. Rick and TJ formed and instant strong bond that melted my heart. I juggled homeschooling both TJ and Jack. Everything was fine.

35

IN THE DESERT

The Lord said to Moses, "I have heard the grumbling of
the Israelites. Tell them, 'At twilight you will eat meat,
and in the morning you will be filled with bread. Then
you will know that I am the Lord your God.'"

—Exodus 16:11–12

October 2020–November 2020

In early October, Lorraine tested positive for COVID-19 two days
after we were around her. An anxiety-filled fourteen-day quarantine
followed, but fortunately all four of us tested negative and none of us
developed symptoms.

I tried not to notice Jack's increasing need for help, especially
writing papers. He was in middle school now, I reasoned; he had a
heavy workload. It was overwhelming, even for me. Missing school
due to quarantine caused him to fall behind and raised the stress
level.

Almost a year to the date of Jack's last flare and three weeks
after the COVID exposure, Jack couldn't write a paper. I caught him
online talking to Owen when he was supposed to be working on a
paper. As a result, I told him to come downstairs to work in the dining room turned classroom.

"You're so mean!" Jack screamed at me. He stormed back to his room.

I found him in his bed crying into a pillow. "Come on downstairs, Jack."

"Why?"

"I don't want you in your room all day. Come down and sit at the dining room table so I can help both you and TJ."

"No! TJ's too loud."

"Then go downstairs in the office and work with Dad. You can use my desk and my really comfortable chair."

"Why can't I work in here?"

"You weren't working. You were talking with Owen."

"Oh my gosh!"

"Since you're overwhelmed with the paper, why don't we start on something easier? Come downstairs and label your Civil War map."

"Mom, that's not easy."

"Okay, well, I'll help you with it. Putting it off won't help."

"Mom, stop."

"Jack, come on. Let's get it done. You can do it."

"Oh my gosh, Mom! Stop! I am literally having a mental breakdown right now. Leave me alone!"

I retreated down to the basement to "cash in" on our agreement that when one of us was reaching the end of our sanity the other stepped in. While Luke was working long hours in the city, this was rarely an option for me. I was glad to have him home. Luke went up to Jack's room while I returned to the classroom to work with TJ on his spelling. Five or ten minutes went by and Jack quieted.

"Hope?" Luke called down to me. "Can you come up here, please?"

"I'll be right back, TJ. Can you draw an up-close picture of the sun with sunspots for me?"

Thankfully, TJ began to draw a large circle on the paper I'd given him. I went upstairs to Jack's room.

Luke was sitting on the edge of Jack's bed. He looked at me, his eyes pained and weary. "Jack's been having suicidal thoughts," he said without preamble.

I momentarily froze. Jack was still lying on the bed, but he'd stopped crying. I scooted Jack's wobble stool over to the head of his bed and put a hand on his arm. "How long have you been having these thoughts, Jack?"

Jack sniffed. "I guess they started on Monday."

I thought back to Monday—two days ago. It had marked the boys' return to school after our fourteen-day quarantine. Jack had been cranky. He'd stalled getting ready. I'd assumed it was due to being tired. He'd seemed fine that afternoon.

"Jack, you know you can talk to us if you're having those thoughts. It's important not to keep those thoughts to yourself."

Given our family history, we'd spoken previously about how to handle suicidal thoughts and the importance of talking about them. Jack had said he didn't want to live anymore back when he was seven. Upon further discussion, it had become clear that seven-year-old Jack didn't understand the gravity of those words and the meaning behind them. I was fairly confident at eleven he knew exactly what it meant. Either way, the pain of hearing your child—the child to whom you gave life—say he doesn't want to live anymore—is indescribable. I felt like I couldn't breathe.

"Do you know what made you feel that way?" I asked.

"Schoolwork. It's so much, and it will always be there. I want to get away from it."

"How would you do it?" It caused a pang in my stomach to ask that question, but my psychology background had taught me it was essential to assess whether or not there was a plan.

Jack shrugged. "I don't know."

I exhaled. "Jack, I know sixth grade is tough and you're still getting used to the added work. I know it can be overwhelming and seem like there's no end in sight. But really, school is a small percentage of your whole life."

Luke rubbed Jack's arm. "We love you, bud. We want you to be here with us. You have a whole lot of life left—a lot of amazing things." He cleared his throat.

"I have so much to do. I'll never catch up."

"We'll help you," Luke said. "It's not the end of the world if it's late."

"Do you want me to see if you can talk to Seth today?" I asked.

"No, it's okay. I can talk to him on Friday."

"Is it okay if I touch base with him? Can I tell him what you told us?"

"Yeah, that's fine. I was going to tell him anyway."

"Good. It's important to be as honest as possible with him, and with us. You know, I wasn't supposed to be able to have you. You're very special, and God has an important purpose for you."

Jack reached for a tissue from the box on his desk and blew his nose. "I know. I just don't feel like doing anything."

TJ appeared in the doorway. "Mom, I drew like ten drawings of the sun, the planets, *and* the dwarf planets. What should I do now?"

"You can go help TJ now, Mom," Jack said. "Thank you for listening."

"Of course, Jack. Make sure you always talk to us if you have those thoughts. You know you can tell us anything."

"I know."

"We're always here for you, bud," Luke said. "We love you."

"Love you."

"Mom, what can I do?" TJ asked.

After leaving a text message and voicemail on Seth's cell phone, I managed to get TJ through the remainder of his spelling and science. I also made Jack an appointment with a pediatric psychiatrist to discuss medication options. We'd considered psychotropic medication for Jack previously, but we'd wanted to finish the PANDAS treatment first. The soonest appointment was two weeks out, but it was a plan. The question remained; was this a flare?

*****

I worked with Jack for the remainder of the afternoon with little to no progress. After sitting with him for a half hour in front of his computer trying to coach him through the introduction of his paper, Jack was yelling and screaming that he didn't know what to write. Sometimes it helped to switch gears, so we headed downstairs to watch his video for fallacies.

After viewing the video, the assignment was to write four examples of different fallacies on notecards. On the surface, fallacies was the perfect class for Jack. He understood fallacies well, but when it came time to write out the notecards, Jack declared that school was stupid and pointless. By dinner time, he was lying on the couch.

"I hate school! I don't want to live anymore!"

Hearing those words tore my heart out. I tried so hard to give my kids a good, happy life. It's what every parent wants.

A few hours earlier, Seth had retuned my call between appointments. He advised me that it sounded liked Jack's suicidal ideation was about escaping school. He asked if Jack had concrete plans to act on those thoughts. He advised me to keep a close eye on Jack and we'd talk further at Jack's appointment on Friday, or sooner if necessary.

"You hate your life, or you hate school?" I asked, attempting to break Jack out of his black and white thinking.

"School *is* my life."

"It's not. I know it seems like it is, but it's not. Right now, you might be learning a lot of things you don't care about, but this is the foundation. Most of school at this stage is giving you skills and teaching you how to learn. It seems like school is forever, but as you move on, you'll have more opportunity to learn about what you're interested in—especially in college, should you choose that path. I felt just like you in grammar school, but I loved high school."

I wasn't sure how much of my speech Jack was absorbing, but one thing was clear: we weren't getting any schoolwork done. We let Jack retreat to his room with strict instructions to leave the door open.

"Mom, what's wrong with Jack?" TJ asked. "Will he be okay?"

I hugged him. "He will be okay. We're taking care of him. Jack has something called PANDAS. Do you remember how he had the procedure done with the IV last year?"

TJ shook his head.

"Well, that procedure helped, but sometimes when Jack gets sick or is exposed to an illness, he has a flare."

"What's a fare?"

It means Jack's immune system, which is what your body uses to fight sickness, affects his brain. It can cause him to feel sad, angry, and unable to do his schoolwork."

"So is the fare because we were exposed to COVID?"

A lightbulb went off in my head when I heard my brilliant boy's question. I'd believed God; I'd trusted him. I'd been confident we'd celebrate a year flare-free. Yet COVID was a novel virus. Maybe exposure to it had caused this. Even though he'd tested negative, maybe his immune system fighting it off had tipped off a flare.

"Do you think we should keep him home from school tomorrow?" I asked Luke. "I feel like he needs a mental health day."

"I think Jack needs a one-day break," TJ chimed in.

"I trust you, hun," Luke said. "He can take the day off tomorrow as long as he understands this won't be a regular thing. We have to be clear with the expectation that he catches up over the weekend."

I went upstairs and relayed the information to Jack. He seemed relieved. I texted Charlotte and relayed what was going on with Jack.

"I'm so sorry," she texted back. "I'm praying it's short-lived. You can buy a strep test off Amazon. It might be worth testing at home. Then if it's positive you can take him to the doctor and say he has a sore throat. I'll pick TJ up in the morning."

After Charlotte picked up TJ the next morning, I drove to Chick-fil-A to get Jack his favorite breakfast—mini chicken and biscuit sandwiches, hash browns, and orange juice.

"Hi, Mom," Jack called from upstairs when I got home.

"Hi, sweetie. How are you feeling?"

"Better. I think I just needed a day off. Where did you go?"

"Chick-fil-A. I got breakfast."

"Yes! Thank you, thank you, thank you!" Jack bounded down the stairs.

After breakfast, Jack and I prepared for our small, outdoor socially distanced Halloween party that Saturday. For some reason, the worry, sadness, and disappointment hit me all at once. I tried to sneak away and hide my tears from Jack, but he saw them anyway.

"What's wrong, Mom?"

"I'm fine, sweetie. I just don't want you to feel this way. I didn't think you'd have another flare."

"Well, Mom, I don't know if it's really a flare. I think I'm just stressed out and needed a break. I feel better today, but I promise I'll tell you if I'm having those thoughts, okay?" He hugged me. "Why don't you do some writing now? Work on the PANDAS book. I'm going to edit a video anyway. I'll leave my door open."

I didn't want Jack to have to comfort me, but at the same time I was encouraged by his display of compassion and maturity. I tried to write, but I couldn't force words onto the page. After all, I was writing a story of hope. I was writing about God keeping His promises. I was questioning. I felt discouraged. I couldn't write.

*****

On Friday, Jack still couldn't write his paper. We struggled through fallacies and finally got it done. I took him to his appointment with Seth.

"I want to be careful how I say this because I don't want you to take it the wrong way," Seth said, "But if you started having the thoughts on Monday or Tuesday, what made you bring them up on Wednesday? Was it your schoolwork?"

"Yeah, I guess." Jack bounced on the couch. "I guess they got stronger."

"Okay, that's fair. What can you do when you have those thoughts?"

"I can talk about them and also distract myself. I think I just needed a break."

"I'm glad you realize that. I'm encouraged that you know how to handle the thoughts. Let's keep an eye on this, okay?"

Jack spent Saturday morning making signs and getting things ready for the party. "What else can I do to help, Mom?" he asked.

I smiled. That day he was so…present. "Why don't you draw a face on your pumpkin? Then you can clean the table outside."

"I'll do the table while TJ works on his pumpkin. What spray should I use?"

Jack sprayed the table while TJ drew a mouth with two teeth, a triangle nose and eyes, and slanted eyebrows on the pumpkin he named "Tall Guy". Jack had opted to get a pumpkin from the grocery store instead of the pumpkin patch because it was cheaper and "it just doesn't make sense to spend that much more, Mom." Frugal, like his father.

Jack drew a happy face on his pumpkin, and I set to work carving and scooping. Jack swept the leaves off the deck, made lunch for himself and TJ, helped me put up the decorations, and set out the prepackaged snacks. "Anything else I can help you with, Mom?" he asked.

"I think we're all set, sweetie. Thanks for all of your help."

"Well, I mean, you're having the party for TJ and me. It would be pretty rude if I didn't help." He smiled.

I felt myself getting emotional. I gave Jack a side hug. "Sorry it's more subdued than our usual Halloween parties."

"Mom. I'm just glad I get to see friends."

I helped the boys into their costumes. TJ was Cat Boy from *PJ Masks* and Jack was a crewmate from the game, *Among Us*, with a green blow up costume. Even our dog had a shiny green gecko costume. Soon after, a handful of guests arrived and followed Jack's signs directing them to the backyard. The kids had a blast, enjoying snacks and a Halloween candy scavenger hunt. When the party was over, I realized something. The kids didn't care that we had a smaller party and no cupcakes decorated as spiders. It didn't matter that we didn't have pizza. It didn't matter that we had a scavenger hunt and free play instead of organized crafts and games. It didn't even matter that everyone had to stay outside and keep masks on. The kids had fun anyway.

It was a good reminder at a time when nothing felt normal. I enjoyed making Halloween treats and going all out for the kids' Halloween parties, but I stressed a lot too. We put a lot of pressure on ourselves as moms and dads. We love our children so much; we want them to be happy. We desperately want them to have good days, good parties, and good memories. Our kids don't crave or need perfection; they just need us to keep showing up. The beautifully frosted cupcakes, handmade costumes, and swept floors are nice, but they're extras.

*****

On Sunday morning Luke began helping Jack with his paper. I heard the two of them conducting research on the topic while I played Hot Wheels with TJ. It sounded like Jack was cooperating. My phone dinged, indicating a text. It was from Charlotte.

"How's Jack doing?"

"Much better! He's working on his paper now."

"Great! Believe me, I know the PTSD that comes along with this."

I knew exactly what she meant. It's the eggshells under your feet with every step. It's the questions running through your head. *Is this the way it's always going to be? Is it just a bad day? How can I help? When will it get better? Is it my fault?* I'd read too many accounts on the PANDAS board of parents dealing with their own trauma responses.

I vividly remember one night when Jack was nine, and he had a big rage over bedtime. He'd pushed me, and Luke needed to hold him until he finally fell asleep from pure exhaustion. In the dark hours of early morning, I awoke to Jack standing in my doorway. I felt instant fear, followed by guilt for my initial reaction. Jack was confused after passing out in the middle of a rage. He didn't understand why we hadn't read books. He spent the rest of the night in our bed.

Jack did his research with Luke, but his cooperation didn't last. By dinner time, he'd written one sentence. Luke tried to help him again after dinner but came down near tears after thirty minutes.

"I'm not getting through to him. It's like nothing I'm saying is going in."

I embraced him. "Do you think it's a flare?" I asked into Luke's shoulder.

"I don't know if it's a flare or stress from school."

"He could be flaring from the COVID exposure, I just…I thought this wouldn't happen anymore after the IVIG."

"Why don't you contact Dr. K in the morning? Maybe he needs to be put back on antibiotics." Jack had recently finished his one-year prescription.

I went upstairs to check on Jack. He was lying in bed. "I made Dad sad," he wailed when he saw me.

"Dad just wants you to work hard. You know how hard Dad works, right?"

"Yeah."

"He wants to help you. He wants you to be successful. Why don't you hop back on your wobble stool and we'll try to make some headway on your paper? You've done all the research. Now we just need to organize your thoughts."

"I don't remember anything from my research, though."

"Well, did you take notes?"

"No."

I sighed. "Jack, Dad told you to take notes."

"Oh my gosh!"

"Jack, come on, you need to take notes. Remember how I told you a big part of school is learning skills? Taking notes is an important skill. That's how I learned to write: I took notes at the writers' conferences. Now I have notebooks full of notes to refer back to."

"Yeah, but I don't know how to do that, though."

"Remember, I taught you how to find the main ideas and jot down bullet points?"

Jack stared at me blankly. His pupils were dilated, though not as significantly as they had been during prior flares. My shoulders and neck began to tense up. We'd been over this dozens of times. Jack and I struggled through his introduction.

"Good job. Now remember, the three body paragraphs are your three main points. Let's outline them. Then we need three to five sentences about each point or idea."

"Why three body paragraphs?"

"Because it's a five-paragraph paper. That means an introduction, three body paragraphs, and a conclusion." I felt like I was teaching Jack how to write a paper for the first time. "What are your three main ideas?"

"Mom, I don't know!"

"What's one interesting thing you learned from your research?"

"I don't know. Nothing."

"Don't yell at me. It's ten thirty at night, and I'm sitting here trying to help you with this paper you've had all day to do."

"I was researching."

"All day?"

"Yes!"

"If you were researching all day, you must remember something. Name one fact you learned, and we'll go from there."

"I don't know, Mom! On my gosh!"

"Okay, let's review the writing prompt again."

"Mom, stop it! I know what the stupid prompt is. I don't know what to write!"

A lot of this conversation sounds like typical middle school arguing. Some of it might have been. Jack was clearly stuck, though. We talked in this circle for endless minutes. I helped Jack formulate some semblance of an outline using my writing website. Halfway through the first paragraph, both Jack and I were exhausted. Jack's lids were drooping. I checked the time. It was eleven thirty.

"Bud, why don't we stop for tonight? We're both exhausted. I'll help you finish it after HH tomorrow."

"But I have to stream at four tomorrow."

"You'll get home by two thirty. You'll have time. We have the outline done."

"No, I need to finish it tonight."

I wanted to get the never-ending paper done too, but I could feel my brain going into sleep mode, and I was having trouble keeping my eyes open. Maybe if I just laid down for a little bit…

"How about if we take a little rest, and I'll set my alarm for a half-hour from now?"

Jack didn't take much convincing. "Okay," he said as he crawled into bed, "but make sure you wake me."

I set my alarm for midnight and squeezed into the twin bed next to Jack. I was conflicted; Jack needed sleep, but if he didn't get the paper done, he'd be faced with another paper and he'd fall behind again, leading to more stress. I also knew Jack needed time after school to wind down and stream with his friends. I didn't have much time to contemplate it. Within moments I fell into a deep sleep. When my alarm went off, I only half-woke before turning it off. The next morning, Jack awoke furious with me.

"Why didn't you wake me? You were supposed to wake me."

"I'm sorry, I shut my alarm off and fell right back to sleep."

"You promised you'd wake me."

"I'm sorry, but we both needed sleep. I'll help you finish the paper after school, before you stream."

"I won't have time."

"You have to finish it before you stream."

"This is so unfair. I'm getting punished for your actions."

"You had all day yesterday to do your paper. We'll talk about it more after school. Now get ready. Rick's mom will be here in twenty-five minutes."

Jack stomped into the bathroom. I retreated downstairs to pack lunches. Jack was still in the bathroom when Charlotte pulled into the driveway. I quickly updated her.

"Bye, Mom." TJ pulled on his backpack and hurried out the door, anxious to see Rick and dive into a conversation about Minecraft.

"Jack, come on," I called up the stairs. "Mrs. Costapolis is waiting."

"I'm getting dressed."

"Now? What have you been doing for the last half hour?"

It was another five minutes before Jack emerged from the bathroom. Once Charlotte pulled away, I sat at the kitchen table and put my head in my hands.

"I'm sure Charlotte understands," Luke said.

"It's not that." My shoulders heaved. "It's the way he talks to me when he's like this. It feels like he hates me." Perhaps I was being a bit dramatic, but I was worn thin and bitterly disappointed.

"You know that's not him. What did Dr. K say?"

"He said Jack only needs antibiotics with a positive strep test. If the strep test is negative, the symptoms should resolve on their own in a week or two. The strep test I took was negative, but I'm not sure I got a good enough sample. I'll try it again. If the symptoms don't resolve, I'll take him to the doctor and say he has a sore throat. I'd like to avoid going to the doctor if possible, with COVID."

Jack was sullen on the drive home, in contrast to TJ and Rick's excited chatter.

"Iron golems will attack you if you punch villagers," TJ said.

"Really?" Rick said.

I smiled at their conversation. After dropping Rick home, the paper struggle continued. Jack insisted I was punishing him. I tried to get him on track. He stomped his feet, yelling, "I don't know!" every time I tried to prompt him. "You're mean!"

I threw up my hands. "I need a minute."

Jack ran to the top of the stairs and yelled something at me as I retreated. I don't remember what it was, but it was the last straw. "Your illness does not give you the right to be a jerk," I fired back, regretting the words the instant they left my mouth. "I'm sorry. I need a minute."

I retreated to my sanctuary—my corner of the office—and sat in my ridiculously comfortable chair until the boiling anger and bitter frustration eased. By the time I returned to his room, Jack had also calmed down. I sat on the edge of his bed. "I'm sorry I said you were being a jerk."

Jack shrugged. "That's okay. I kind of was."

"Let's move on. Let's get this paper done."

Two hours, more crying, and several interruptions from TJ later, the never-ending paper was done. I gave Jack a hug. "I'm proud of you."

"I feel so much better now that it's done. You were right, Mom. Thanks for helping me."

"That's what I'm here for. Let's go downstairs and do that strep test. Then you can have computer time."

I brought Jack into the basement and sat him in my comfy chair. Luke helped by holding his head. I swished the Q-tip in his throat and read the instructions carefully. The test showed negative. I couldn't be certain of its accuracy, so if Jack didn't improve, I'd take him to the doctor.

*****

Jack did improve and quickly. The day after the paper completion, Jack did his work without complaint. He reported feeling more like himself and less overwhelmed. It was a huge relief when he reported that his suicidal thoughts had passed. Even TJ noticed Jack was back to himself.

"Mom, is the fare over?" he asked.

"Yes, I think so, TJ. We need to thank God."

I thanked God. Dr. K had been right as usual. The flare was short-lived. On Monday, Jack had a virtual appointment with the psychiatrist. He started Jack on a low dose of an antidepressant. Fortunately, the pill was small, flat, and easy to swallow. Jack had no side effects from the medication. I noticed he was falling asleep more easily. Over the next few weeks, things continued to improve. We were back to baseline.

36

THE CHRISTMAS MIRACLE

Stay here for now, and may the Lord help you keep your promise.

—1 Samuel 1:23

Friday, November 27, 2020

We had Thanksgiving with just the four of us. While we missed seeing family, we enjoyed a low-key day. Once dinner was complete, we played Jeremy Camp's Christmas album on Spotify while we cleaned the kitchen. Then the four of us retired to the family room to have popcorn and watch *Mr. Popper's Penguins*.

"We read *Mr. Popper's Penguins* in first grade," TJ said. "I like it."

"I'm not sure if I'll like this movie or not," Jack said between mouthfuls of popcorn, "but I'll try it."

"Sounds like a realistic plot," I joked. "A man is randomly mailed a crate full of penguins. Not to mention, how did they survive the flight?"

Luke laughed. "Okay, writer."

Soon we were all laughing as we watched Jim Carey's apartment get flooded.

"I *do* like this movie," Jack said. "Good pick, Dad."

"See, I told you it was funny, Jack. My teacher read us *Mr. Poppers Penguins* in first grade, and I laughed," TJ said.

After the movie, Jack read to TJ and put him to bed. The following day we stuck with tradition and put up our Christmas decorations.

"Mom, can we play with the graham crackers?" TJ asked when we unloaded the two bins of nutcrackers I'd collected over the years.

"Yes, as long as we're gentle."

TJ and I played for a while, while Jack helped Luke take down pictures to make room for our obscene amount of Christmas decorations. I took the dogs for a walk and played a game of war with TJ. After dinner, the four of us put up the remainder of the Christmas decorations, the kids squealing and laughing at our singing stuffed Christmas tree and snowmen as though seeing them for the first time.

"Hey, Jack, remember last year when you kept insisting on going to Walgreens to buy more Christmas lights, and I finally said, 'This is the last time we're going to Walgreens this year'?" I teased.

Jack giggled. "Yeah, because you kept not buying enough to do the whole bush. You were like, 'Okay, hunny, that's enough. I'm not going to Walgreens again.'"

"I do not sound like that." I laughed at Jack's high-pitched voice.

"Don't worry, this year we're getting a ton more lights," he said.

"Hun, Waverly turned into a reindeer," Luke called from the family room.

"Let me see! Let me see!" the kids shouted.

I laughed and grabbed my phone to take pictures of our big Great Pyrenees mix lounging on the couch wearing a headband of blue antlers. After that, TJ challenged Jack to a game of war.

"Sure," Jack said. "TJ, you can't look at your cards. That's cheating."

I prepared myself to mediate a fight, but I soon heard laughing and good-natured ribbing. I'm not sure if anyone actually won the game because TJ and Jack moved on to chasing each other up and down the stairs with a stuffed Minecraft sword. The sounds of them laughing and screaming filled the house and my heart.

Jack and TJ played together for the rest of the night without fighting or rigidity. I sat down on the couch next to Luke.

"It's so nice to hear the kids laughing and playing together."

"It is," he answered. "It's a Christmas miracle."

He wasn't being facetious. For us, any length of free play and unmediated interaction between our boys was, in fact, a miracle. Having Jack back was a miracle. Seeing TJ seek his brother's attention appropriately was a miracle.

I'd learned to savor these moments. This isn't the end of our story. I can't guarantee Jack won't have another flare, but I do believe the IVIG was a success. His last flare was much milder and more short-lived. We do have antibiotics and Prednisone on hand in case of another flare. I've seen more patience, grace, and peace from Jack than I once thought possible. But nothing is impossible with God.

Over the years, I've heard people question (and questioned myself) why God allows us to endure pain and hardships. We can't always know the answer to that question, but I do believe that God is sovereign. God is our heavenly Father. As a parent, I put Jack through surgery and IVIG. It hurt my heart to do so, just as I believe it hurts God's heart to watch His children suffer. We let Jack go through this because we believed it was what he needed to heal. God works in our own lives in ways we can't possibly see or understand.

Being Jack and TJ's mom has taught me to manage my expectations, pick my battles, and count my blessings. Most importantly, I've learned that even though we may have to wait, in God's time God keeps His promises.

AUTHOR'S NOTE

I understand that the diagnosis of PANDAS (and related PANS) is still a highly controversial and contentious clinical issue, and that either of these diagnoses has not gained wide acceptance within the medical community.

The above words were taken from a page we had to sign at the surgical center when Jack was receiving his IVIG. I'm working to change that, but I can't do it alone. PANDAS is real: it's childhood-robbing, it's life-altering, it's serious. And it's treatable—maybe even curable. Children and their families are suffering. Parents are being told that their children have autism, OCD, anxiety, depression, even schizophrenia. These disorders exist in their own right. Still, all over the world children are suffering, with many receiving band-aid treatments or even being institutionalized. Parents are being turned away or blamed by counselors, physicians, and family members. The medical community is failing our children. They can do better, and they won't silence my voice. Don't let them silence yours either. Mothers will be the ones to change the world.

(One hundred percent of profits from this book will be donated to the PANDAS Network to further research PANDAS, PANS, and AE, and to offer financial help to families struggling to afford treatment for their children.)

About the Author

Hope Shepherd is a special needs homeschooling mom of two boys. She discovered writing on a frigid night holed up with a newborn, a precocious three-year-old, and a travelling husband. Hope is passionate in her mission to raise awareness of PANDAS (pediatric autoimmune neuropsychiatric disorders associated with strep). She is also a fierce advocate for autism, ADHD, and mental health. Hope seeks to raise awareness and remove stigma surrounding mental health and neurodiversity.

Hope has a degree in clinical psychology. When she's not writing or homeschooling, she spends time involved in various church ministries. She is a contributing author for The Mighty website and also shares a YouTube channel (Sonny Mom Inc.) with her eleven-year-old son. Hope lives in the Chicago suburbs with her husband, two sons, two large, vocal dogs, and an equally introverted cat.

Printed in the USA
CPSIA information can be obtained
at www.ICGtesting.com
LVHW080750110424
776968LV00014B/656

9 781638 145745